Wearable KnitWits

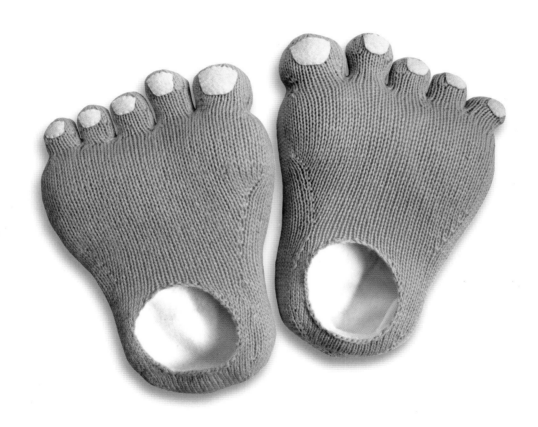

Wearable KnitWits

20 Fun Designs to Knit for Adults & Kids

KATIE BOYETTE

SELLERS
PUBLISHING

Published by **Sellers Publishing, Inc.**
161 John Roberts Road, South Portland, Maine 04106

Visit our Web site: www.sellerspublishing.com
E-mail: rsp@rsvp.com

Design and layout copyright © 2012 BlueRed Press Ltd
Text copyright © 2012 Katie Boyette
Patterns and templates copyright © 2012 Katie Boyette
All rights reserved.
Design by Matt Windsor

ISBN 13: 978-1-4162-0845-7
Library of Congress Number 2012931315

10 9 8 7 6 5 4 3 2 1

Printed and Bound in China

Knitting Needle Sizes

Metric (mm)	U.S.
2.0	0
2.25	1
2.75	2
3.0	-
3.25	3
3.5	4
3.75	5
4.0	6
4.5	7
5.0	8
5.5	9
6.0	10
6.5	10.5
7.0	-
7.5	-
8.0	11
9.0	13
10.0	15
12.75	17
15.0	19
19.0	35
25.0	50

courtesy of the Craft Yarn Council, Gastonia, N.C.

Contents

Introduction

After writing two books of toy patterns, I'm excited to take a totally new direction: wearables.

I've always loved knitting hats, mittens, sweaters and other cozy things for my kids and friends. A couple of years ago, I decided to knit a pair of slippers that looked like giant feet. They were an instant hit! The slippers sent my kids into fits of giggles and friends all wanted pairs of their own. Best of all, they're actually really warm and cozy on our cold wooden floors in the winter. It was a perfect combination of silliness and functionality (just like me!). So I thought, yes, this is the new direction I want to go. In this book you'll find patterns that are cute, stylish, or just downright silly, but they're all designed to elicit a smile.

The best part about designing for this book is that I get to use all the techniques I love – techniques I rarely get to use when knitting toys. There are patterns with cables, fair isle, double knitting, and lots of color work. I love challenging knitters to try something new, so don't be afraid to try your hand at a new trick. Thanks to the Internet, there are endless resources for knitters. If you get stuck on a step, ask someone at your local yarn shop, or look up a video on the Web. There are thousands of knitters locally and online who would love to help you expand your arsenal of knitting techniques. I count myself among those helpful knitters, so feel free to address any questions, as well as compliments, complaints, or interesting life anecdotes to katie@caffaknitted.com. Happy knitting!

Katie Boyette

Head Knitwits

Bluetooth Hat
Hooter Hat

Bluetooth Hat

I'm assuming that if you have children, they occasionally act like little monsters. Perhaps your significant other has been known to act like one as well? Then why not dress them like monsters? If you enjoyed the toys from the first two Knitwit books, this hat is the best way to turn yourself or your child into living amigurumi. This hat is knit from the top down, and has cozy ear flaps. The garter stitch border keeps the edge from curling, and holds the hat in place, but the yarn is stretchy enough to grow with your child.

Materials

- 1 skein Cascade Pacific in 39 blue (MC)
- 1 skein Cascade Cherub DK in 01 white (CC)
- 1 set US size 7 (4.5 mm) double pointed needles
- 1 US size 5 (3.75 mm) 18 in. circular needle
- Stitch marker
- Yarn needle
- Embroidery needle

Toy stuffing
Scraps of felt in white, black, and blue
Thread in white, black, and blue

Finished head circumference:
3–6 mths – 17 in.
6–12 mths – 18 in.
1–3 yrs – 19½ in.
4–young adult – 21 in.

Gauge:
20 sts and 24 rows over 4 in. in stockinette st using larger needles

Glossary of abbreviations

CC – contrasting color
CO – cast on
k – knit
k2tog – decrease by knitting two together
kfb – increase by knitting into front and back of stitch
MC – main color
pm – place marker
ssk – decrease by slip one, slip one, knit slipped stitches together
st[s] – stitch[es]

Knit from the top down
Using US size 7 (4.5 mm) double pointed needles and MC, CO 6 [6, 6, 6], pm, join to knit in the round.
Round 1: Kfb 6 times. 12 [12, 12, 12] sts.
Round 2: (Kfb, k1) 6 times. 18 [18, 18, 18] sts.
Round 3: (Kfb, k2) 6 times. 24 [24, 24, 24] sts.
Round 4: (kfb, k3) 6 times. 30 [30, 30, 30] sts.
Round 5: Knit.
Continue increasing 6 sts evenly every other round until you have 78 [84, 90, 96] sts.
Switch to US size 7 (4.5 mm) circular needle if desired.
Knit even for 2 [2½, 3, 3½] in.

Begin dividing for earflaps: Place 9 [11, 11, 13] sts on scrap yarn for back of hat, place the next 15 [15, 17, 17] sts on a double pointed needle for first ear flap, place the next 30 [32, 34, 38] sts on scrap yarn for front, place the next 15 [15, 17, 17] sts on a double pointed needle for second ear flap, place remaining 9 [11, 11, 13] sts on scrap yarn for back of hat.

Begin ear flaps
Using US size 7 (4.5 mm) double pointed needle and using MC, begin first ear flap by knitting across right side. 15 [15, 17, 17] sts
Knit 6 [6, 8, 8] more rows in stockinette st. Next row: K1, k2tog, k9 [9, 11, 11], ssk, k1. 13 [13, 15, 15] sts

Next row: Purl.
Next row: K1, k2tog, k7 [7, 9, 9], ssk, k1. 11 [11, 13, 13] sts
Next row: Purl.
Continue decreasing 2 sts every other row until 5 [5, 7, 7] sts. remain. Place sts on stitch holder. Repeat for second flap.

Border
Using US size 5 (3.75 mm) circular needle and CC, pick up and knit 9 [11, 11, 13] sts from first piece of scrap yarn, pick up 6 [6, 7, 7] sts along edge of ear flap, knit the 5 [5, 7, 7] sts at bottom edge of ear flap, pick up and knit 6 [6, 7, 7] sts along other edge of ear flap, knit the next 30 [32, 34, 38] sts from scrap yarn for front, pick up 6 [6, 7, 7] sts along edge of

second ear flap, knit the 5 [5, 7, 7] sts at bottom edge of ear flap, pick up and knit 6 [6, 7, 7] sts along other edge of ear flap, knit the remaining 9 [11, 11, 13] sts from scrap yarn for back of hat.

Place marker, join to knit in the round (see figure 1). 82 [88, 98, 106] sts

Knit 1 round.

Purl 1 round.

Bind off. Weave in loose ends.

Eyes (make 2)

Using US size 7 (4.5 mm) double pointed needles and blue, CO 6 [6, 6, 6], pm, join to knit in the round.

Round 1: Kfb 6 times. 12 [12, 12, 12] sts

Round 2: (Kfb, k1) 6 times. 18 [18, 18, 18] sts

Round 3: (Kfb, k2) 6 times. 24 [24, 24, 24] sts

Round 4: Knit.

Round 5: (Kfb, k3) 6 times. 30 [30, 30, 30] sts

Rounds 6–10: Knit.

Round 11: (K2tog, k3) 6 times. 24 [24, 24, 24] sts

Round 12: Knit.

Round 13: (K2tog, k2) 6 times. 18 [18, 18, 18] sts

Rounds 14–15: Knit.

Bind off, leaving a 12 in. tail for seaming.

Stuff eyes firmly with stuffing.

Place hat over head-sized bowl or ball for easy seaming.

Pin eyes into place and sew onto hat (see figure 2).

Cut felt pieces using templates. Sew felt eye pieces onto eyes using corresponding thread color (see figure 3).

Trace outline of eyes with black embroidery floss using a couching stitch, securing in place with a single strand of black thread (see figure 4).

Create mouth using black thread and couching stitch, same as for eye outlines, being careful not to pull sts too tight (see figure 5). Use white thread to sew teeth on upper edge of mouth.

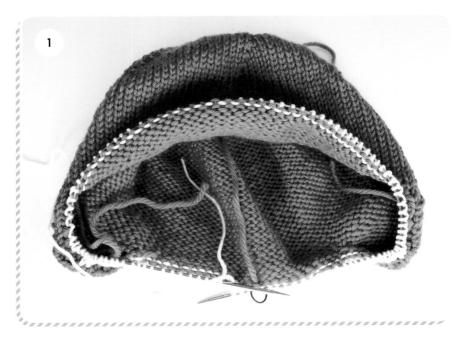

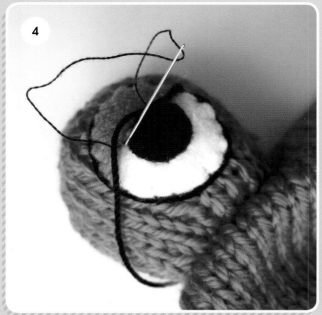

Eyelid (2)

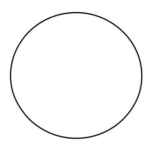

Eyeball (2)

Pupil (2)

Teeth (2)

Hooter Hat

Owls are everywhere now, and there are certainly plenty of hat patterns with owl motifs, but this is only because so many people, myself included, really love owls. I know this is true, because every time I wear this hat, someone asks me to knit one for them. I recently met an owl named Sassy at a wildlife rehab center. She is amazing. It was all I could do not to slip her into my knitting bag and take her home with me. There were two reasons I hesitated. For starters, she's a very large bird of prey, and secondly, I was afraid once we got home, she'd eat my cat.

Materials

- 1 skein Cascade Pacific in 34 gray (MC)
- 1 skein Cascade Pacific in 02 white (CC)
- US size 7 (4.5 mm) double pointed needles
- Yarn needle
- Stitch marker
- Scrap of cardboard or pom pom maker

Finished head circumference:
Child/Adult Small – 20½ in.
Adult Medium – 21½in.
Adult Large – 23in.

Gauge:
20 sts and 24 rows over 4 in. in stockinette st

Glossary of abbreviations

CC – contrasting color
CO – cast on
k – knit
k2tog – decrease by knitting
   two together
MC – main color
p – purl
pm – place marker
st[s] – stitch[es]

Hat

knit from the bottom up: Using MC, CO102 [108, 114] sts., pm, join to knit in the round. Be careful not to twist sts.
Round 1: (K2, p1) 34 [36, 38] times.
Repeat round 1 twice more.
Round 4: (K2 [3, 4], knit first row of chart) 6 times.
Repeat round 4 until chart is completed.
Knit 1 [2, 4] more rounds even.
Next round: (K2tog, k15 [16, 17]) 6 times. 96 [102, 108] sts
Next round: Knit.
Next round: (K2tog, k14 [15, 16]) 6 times. 90 [96, 102] sts
Next round: Knit.
Continue decreasing 6 sts every other round until 30 sts remain, then decrease 6 sts every round until 6 sts remain. Break yarn, pull tail through remaining sts. Weave end into wrong side of hat. Block hat.

Pom pom

You can find pom pom makers at most craft stores, but you can also easily make one yourself if you prefer. Cut a circle of cardboard to the desired diameter of the pom pom.
Mine is 2 in. across. Cut a ½ in. circle in the center of the disk, and cut a slit from the inside circle to outside edge. Cut a length of yarn, and lay it over the center of the disk.
Begin wrapping the desired color of yarn from the inside circle around the outside edge, working your way around the disk (see figure 2). The more yarn you wrap, the fluffier your pom pom will be. Using sharp scissors, cut around the outer edge of the disk. Pull the length of yarn tight and knot to hold pieces of pom pom together. Use the tail to sew to the top of the hat (see figure 3).

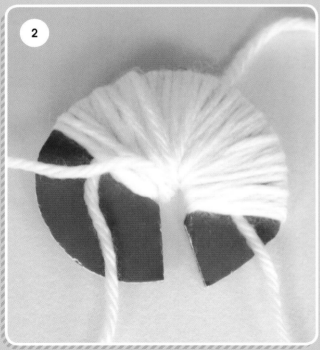

Notes for knitting chart: When changing colors, twist sts together to prevent holes. Run colors along wrong side of hat when not using, twisting every 3rd or 4th st to maintain tension. Knit loosely to avoid puckering sts (see figure 1).

TO KNIT, TO WOO!

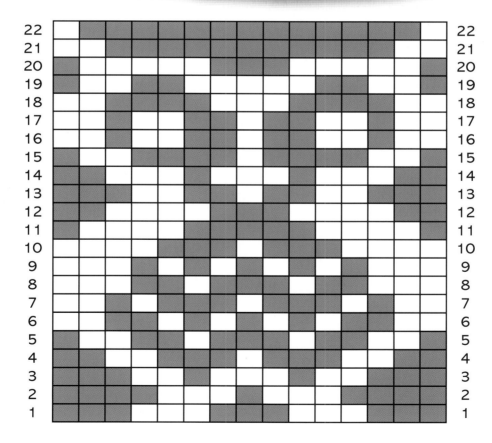

Knitting chart

Neck Knitwits

Mr. Micro Charm

Mr. Micro is the most charming robot you'll ever meet, literally. He's an extremely quick knit, and easy to assemble when you have your beads and tools in front of you. The fun thing about knitted charms is the versatility. You can easily change the size of the charm by changing the yarn and needle size. You can play around with bead colors and shapes. You can put the charm on a chain for a necklace, or attach a ring and use it as a keychain. I like to hook them onto the zipper pulls on my knitting bag. One pack of beads and a skein of yarn will create a lot of Mr Micros. In fact, you could knit him a wife, a few kids, a boss, a mistress, or an army of minions. Who wouldn't want such a cute army of minions?

Materials

- 1 skein Cascade 220 Superwash Sport in 849 blue
- 1 set US size 3 (3.25 mm) double pointed needles
- 2 tiny black buttons
- 1 small pack silver crimp beads
- 1 small pack silver square spacing beads
- 2 short silver tube beads with rings
- 1 silver o-ring
- Small amount of poly stuffing
- Black embroidery floss
- Yarn needle
- Sewing needle
- Scrap of red felt
- Needle nose pliers

Finished size:
3 in.

Gauge:
28 sts and 34 rows over
4 in. in stockinette st

Glossary of abbreviations

CO – cast on
k – knit
k2tog – decrease by knitting
   two together
kfb – increase by knitting into front
   and back of stitch
pm – place marker
st[s] – stitch[es]

Head
CO 6, pm, join to knit in the round.
Round 1: Kfb 6 times. 12 sts
Round 2: (Kfb, k1) 6 times. 18 sts
Rounds 3–6: Knit.
Round 7: (K2tog, k1) 6 times. 12 sts
Pause and stuff head.
Round 8: K2tog 6 times. 6 sts.
Break yarn, pull tail through remaining sts, knot, pull to inside of head.

Body
CO6, pm, join to knit in the round.
Round 1: Kfb 6 times. 12 sts
Round 2: (Kfb, k1) 6 times. 18 sts
Rounds 3–11: Knit.
Round 12: (K2tog, k1) 6 times. 12 sts
Pause and stuff body.
Round 13: K2tog 6 times. 6 sts
Break yarn, pull tail through remaining sts, knot, pull to inside of head.

Assemby

Ears

Using a length of embroidery floss and sewing needle, tie a knot at one end. Insert needle into head through bottom, pull gently until knot pops into fabric. Pull needle out through the center left side where first ear will be. Insert needle through hole at end of tube bead. Insert thread back into head where the ear will be, pulling directly out of the other side for right ear. Pull until tube pops into side of head. Thread second tube bead and repeat (see figure 1). Knot thread at bottom of head once both ears are secure.

Attaching body

Cut a 12 in. length of black embroidery floss. Using sewing needle, insert through bottom of body where first leg will be. Exit needle through center top of body, running through one square bead. Insert needle into center bottom of head, then through center top, through an o-ring, back through center top, through center bottom of head, back through square bead, into top of body, and though bottom at location of second leg (see figure 2). Pull on legs until head is securely attached to body, making sure legs are even. Insert a crimp bead onto each leg thread, and use needle nose pliers to pinch into place. Thread 2 more crimp beads and 1 square bead onto each leg. Knot each leg 1 in. from body, and trim thread.
Pull square bead over knots, and pinch crimp beads at even intervals over legs.

Arms

Cut a 10 in. length of floss. Insert into body at one side for first arm, and directly out of the opposite side for second arm. Insert a crimp bead onto each arm and secure in place next to body. Thread 1 more crimp bead and 1 square bead onto each arm. Knot arms threads 1 in. from body and trim thread. Pull square beads over knots, and pinch crimp beads into place.

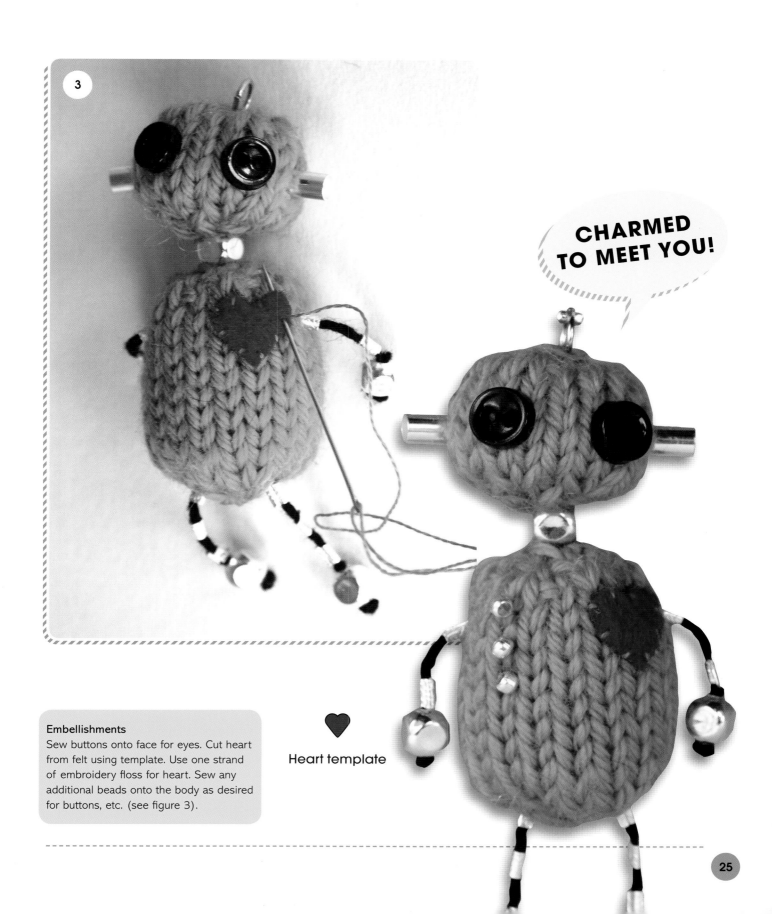

3

CHARMED TO MEET YOU!

Embellishments
Sew buttons onto face for eyes. Cut heart from felt using template. Use one strand of embroidery floss for heart. Sew any additional beads onto the body as desired for buttons, etc. (see figure 3).

Heart template

Feed Me! Bib

My youngest child is now 7 years old, but even years after her days in a high chair, I could still find traces of dinners past, splattered on some remote corner of the wall. The mess was unfathomable. A hungry toddler is truly a monster indeed, but this knitted bib can help. The bib is knitted long to cover a greater area. Cascade Pacific is a machine washable yarn blend. The colors will never fade, and the acrylic portion of the blend will keep the bib from getting too soggy.

Materials

- 1 skein Cascade Pacific in 43 red (MC)
- 1 skein Cascade Pacific in 29 green (CC1)
- 1 skein Cascade Pacific in 48 black (CC2)
- 1 skein Cascade Pacific in 02 white (CC3)
- Scrap of red yarn worsted weight
- US size 7 (4.5 mm) straight needles
- US size 7 (4.5 mm) double pointed needles
- Yarn needle

Finished length:
10½ in.

Gauge:
20 sts and 26 rows over 4 in. in stockinette st.

Glossary of abbreviations

BO – bind off
CC – contrasting color
CO – cast on
k – knit
k2tog – decrease by knitting
two together
MC – main color
pm – place marker
st[s] – stitch[es]

Knit from the bottom up
Using MC and straight needles, CO41 sts.
Rows 1–2: Knit.
Row 3: K4, knit first row of chart, k4.
Row 4: K4, purl next row of chart, k4.
Continue knitting chart with garter st border on edges until chart is complete.
Knit 2 rows.
Begin dividing for shoulders:
Using 1 double pointed needle, k14, BO13; using a second needle, k14. Leave first needle, and continue knitting sts on second needle for right shoulder (see figure 1).

Row 1: Knit.
Row 2: K1, k2tog, k11. 13 sts
Row 3: Knit.
Row 4: K1, k2tog, k10. 12 sts
Row 5: Knit.
Row 6: K1, k2tog, k9. 11 sts
Row 7: Knit.
Row 8: K8, k2tog, k1. 10 sts
Row 9: Knit.
Continue decreasing 1 st shoulder side every other row until 3 sts remain.
Begin knitting i-cord. Knit until i-cord is 12in. long.
Reconnect MC to sts on other double pointed needle, beginning with a wrong side row (see figure 2).

Row 1: Knit. 14 sts
Row 2: K11, k2tog, k1. 13 sts
Row 3: Knit.
Row 4: K10, k2tog, k1. 12 sts
Row 5: Knit.
Row 6: K9, k2tog, k1. 11 sts
Row 7: Knit.
Row 8: K1, k2tog, k8. 10 sts
Row 9: Knit.
Continue decreasing 1 st shoulder side every other row until 3 sts remain.
Begin knitting i-cord. Knit until i-cord is 12in. long.
Weave in all loose ends. Block bib well, press lightly if needed.

1

FEED ME CRUMBS!

Note: When completing chart, wind all contrasting colors into bobbins. Twist sts together when changing colors to prevent holes.

Knitting chart

Badger Scarf

Knitted animal stoles, or vegan stoles if you will, are really popular right now. I came up with the idea for the Badger Scarf after seeing some knitted swatches of Cascade Eco Duo. I thought the gradual color fade would make the perfect palette, and the super soft alpaca blend feels so cozy wrapped around your neck. Badgers may not have the reputation for being very soft and cuddly, but knit one with this yarn, and you may change your mind.

Materials

- 2 skeins Cascade Eco Duo in 1707 light brown (MC)
- 1 skein Cascade Eco Duo in 1705 off white (CC1)
- 1 skein Cascade Eco Duo in 1704 dark gray (CC2)
- 1 skein Cascade Eco Duo in 1708 medium brown (CC3)
- US size 7 (4.5 mm) double pointed needles
- Small piece black felt for nose
- Stitch markers
- Yarn bobbins
- Yarn needle
- Embroidery needle

Finished Size:
65 in. Can be adjusted longer or shorter

Gauge:
18 sts and 24 rows over 4 in. in stockinette st

Glossary of abbreviations

CC – contrasting color
CO – cast on
k – knit
k2tog – decrease by knitting two together
kfb – increase by knitting into front and back of stitch
MC – main color
pm – place marker
ssk – decrease by slip one, slip one, knit slipped stitches together
st[s] – stitch[es]

Note: When working a gradual change between colors, always twist strands to prevent a hole, and run the second color loosely along the inside of the fabric. Keep tension loose to prevent puckering.

Tail

Using CC1, CO4, pm, join to knit in the round.
Round 1: Kfb 4 times. 8 sts
Rounds 2–3: Knit.
Round 4: (Kfb, k2, kfb) twice. 12 sts
Rounds 5–6: Knit.
Round 7: (Kfb, k4, kfb) twice. 16 sts
Rounds 8–9: Knit.
Round 10: (Kfb, k6, kfb) twice. 20 sts
Rounds 11–12: Knit.
Round 13: (Kfb, k8, kfb) twice. 24 sts
Rounds 14–15: Knit.
Round 16: (Kfb, k10, kfb) twice. 28 sts
Rounds 17–18: Knit.
Round 19: (Kfb, k12, kfb) twice. 32 sts
Round 20: Knit.
Begin color transition for tail. Join CC2.

Round 21: (Using CC1 k2, in CC2 k1, in CC1 k5, in CC2 k1, in CC1 k5, in CC2 k1, in CC1 k1) twice.
Round 22: (Using CC1 k1, in CC2 k3, in CC1 k3, in CC2 k3, in CC1 k3, in CC2 k3) twice.
Round 23: (Using CC2 k5, in CC1 k1, in CC2 k5, in CC1 k1, in CC2 k4) twice.
Break CC, weave tail to inside of fabric. Continue working only in CC2.
Rounds 24–26: Knit.
Round 27: (Kfb, k14, kfb) twice. 36 sts
Rounds 28–29: Knit.
Round 30: (Kfb, k16, kfb) twice. 40 sts
Rounds 31–32: Knit.
Round 33: (Kfb, k18, kfb) twice. 44 sts
Rounds 34–42: Knit.
Round 43: (K2tog, k16, ssk) twice. 36 sts

Rounds 44–45: Knit.
Round 46: (K2tog, k12, ssk) twice. 32 sts
Rounds 47–48: Knit.
Round 49: (K2tog, k10, ssk) twice. 28 sts
Add CC3.
Round 50: (K1 in CC3, k4 in CC2) 5 times, k1 in CC3, k2 in CC2.
Round 51: (K1 in CC3, k3 in CC2) 7 times.
Round 52: (K1 in CC3, k2 in CC2) 9 times, k1 in CC3.
Round 53: (K1 in CC3, k1 in CC2) 14 times.
Round 54: (K2 in CC3, k1 in CC2) 9 times. K1 in CC3.
Round 55: (K3 in CC3, k1 in CC2) 7 times.
Continue only in CC3. Knit 4 rounds even.

Break yarn. Place stitches on a length of contrasting scrap yarn.

Back legs (make 2)
Using CC1, CO6, pm, join to knit in the round.
Round 1: (Kfb, k1, kfb) twice. 10 sts
Round 2: Knit.
Round 3: (Kfb, k3, kfb) twice. 14 sts
Round 4: Knit.
Switch to CC2.
Round 5: (Kfb, k5, kfb) twice. 18 sts
Round 6: Knit.
Round 7: (Kfb, k7, kfb) twice. 22 sts
Rounds 8–9: Knit.
Round 10: K9, ssk, k2tog, k9. 20 sts
Round 11: Knit.
Round 12: K8, ssk, k2tog, k8. 18 sts
Round 13: Knit.
Round 14: (K2tog, k5, ssk) twice. 14 sts
Rounds 15–16: Knit.
Switch to CC3.
Round 17: K6, kfb twice, k6. 16 sts
Round 18: K7, kfb twice, k7. 18 sts
Round 19: K2tog, k6, kfb twice, k6, ssk.
Break yarn. Place sts on scrap yarn.
After you have completed both back legs and tail, you will join to continue body. On one double pointed needle, pick up stitches from one side of one leg and slide to end of needle. Follow with the stitches from one side of the tail, and then one side of the other leg. Using another double pointed needle, pick up stitches from legs and body on other side, so the you have the flat back half of the badger split between two needles. Refer to figure 1.
Join yarn in CC3, pm, and begin knitting in the round. 64 sts
Round 1: Knit.
Round 2: (K2tog, k28, ssk) twice. 60 sts
Round 3 and all odd numbered rounds through round 7: Knit.
Round 4: (K2tog, k26, ssk) twice. 56 sts
Round 6: (K2tog, k24, ssk) twice. 52 sts
Round 8: (K2tog, k22, ssk) twice. 48 sts
Knit 4 rounds even. Begin transition to MC.
Round 13: (K1 in MC, k4 in CC3) 5 times, k1 in MC, k2 in CC3.

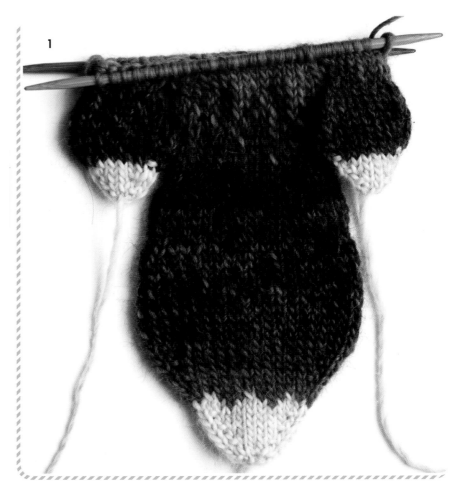

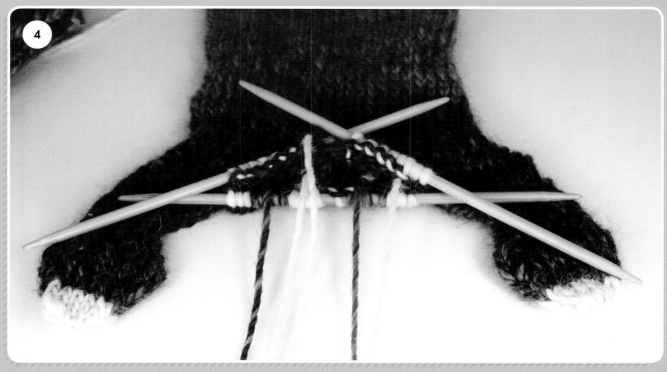

Round 14: (K1 in MC, k3 in CC3) 7 times.
Round 15: (K1 in MC, k2 in CC3)
9 times, k1 in MC.
Round 16: (K1 in MC, k1 in CC3)
14 times.
Round 17: (K2 in MC, k1 in CC3)
9 times. K1 in MC.
Round 18: (K3 in MC, k1 in CC3)
7 times.
Continue only in MC. Knit until scarf is about 14 in. short of the desired length. Transition back to CC3.
Next round: (K1 in CC3, k4 in MC)
5 times, k1 in CC3, k2 in MC.
Next round: (K1 in CC3, k3 in MC)
7 times.
Next round: (K1 in CC3, k2 in MC)
9 times, k1 in CC3.
Next round: (K1 in CC3, k1 in MC)
14 times.
Next round: (K2 in CC3, k1 in MC)
9 times. K1 in CC3.
Next round: (K3 in CC3, k1 in MC)
7 times.
Knit 3 in. in CC3. Begin transition to CC2.
Next round: (K1 in CC2, k4 in CC3)
5 times, k1 in CC2, k2 in CC3.
Next round: (K1 in CC2, k3 in CC3)
7 times.
Next round: (K1 in CC2, k2 in CC3)
9 times, k1 in CC2.
Next round: (K1 in CC2, k1 in CC3)
14 times.
Next round: (K2 in CC2, k1 in CC3)
9 times. K1 in CC2.
Next round: (K3 in CC2, k1 in CC3)
7 times.
Knit 5 rounds in CC2.

Begin end of scarf
Next round: (Kfb, k24, kfb) twice. 52 sts
Next round and every other round to end: Knit.
Next round: (Kfb, k26, kfb) twice. 56 sts
Next round: (Kfb, k28, kfb) twice. 60 sts
Next round: (Kfb, k30, kfb) twice. 64 sts

Begin diving for feet and head
Next round: K9, place 14 sts on a piece of scrap yarn, place the next 18 sts on

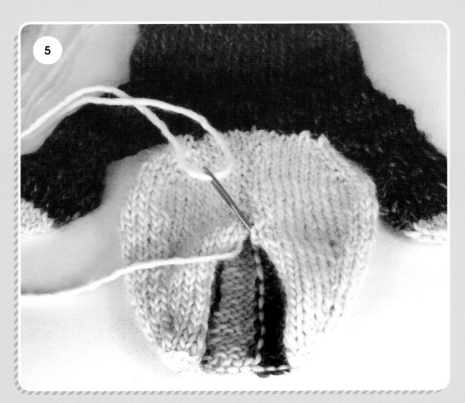

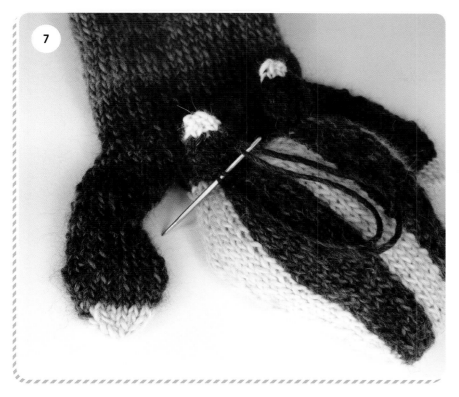

a second piece of scrap yarn, place the next 14 sts on another piece of scrap yarn, k9 (see figure 2). 18 sts

*Round 1: Kfb, k6, ssk, k2tog, k6, kfb. 18 sts
Round 2: K7, ssk, k2tog, k7. 16 sts
Round 3: K6, ssk, k2tog, k6. 14 sts
Rounds 4–5: Knit.
Round 6: K6, kfb twice, k6. 16 sts
Round 7: Knit.
Round 8: K7, kfb twice, k7. 18 sts
Round 9: Knit.
Round 10: (Kfb, k7, kfb) twice. 22 sts
Rounds 11–12: Knit.
Round 13: (K2tog, k7, ssk) twice. 18 sts
Round 14: Knit.
Round 15: (K2tog, k5, ssk) twice. 14 sts
Switch to CC1.
Round 16: Knit.
Round 17: (K2tog, k3, ssk) twice. 10 sts
Round 18: Knit.
Round 19: (K2tog, k1, ssk) twice. 6 sts
Break yarn, pull tail through remaining sts, knot, pull knot to inside of fabric.
Pick up 18 sts from middle piece of scrap yarn, and join CC2 to outside edge. Repeat from * as for first foot. (See figure 3.)

Begin head
The head is worked flat on double pointed needles to create stripes. After completion, it will be seamed up the center of the back.
Place first 14 sts from scrap yarn onto 1 double pointed needle. Split the other sts from the scrap yarn between 2 double pointed needles, 7 on each needle. Create bobbins of yarn to work stripes on head, 3 in CC1, and 2 in CC2. Join CC1 at the center edge of a needle with 7 sts to begin.
Row 1: K11 in CC1, k3 in CC2, k4 in CC1, k3 in CC2, k11 in CC1. (See figure 4.) 28 sts
Row 2 and all even rows: Purl all sts in pattern.
Row 3: (K7, kfb, k2, kfb) in CC1, k3 in CC2, k4 in CC1, k3 in CC2, (kfb, k2, kfb, k7) in CC1. 32 sts
Row 5: (K8, kfb, k2, kfb, k1) in CC1, (kfb,

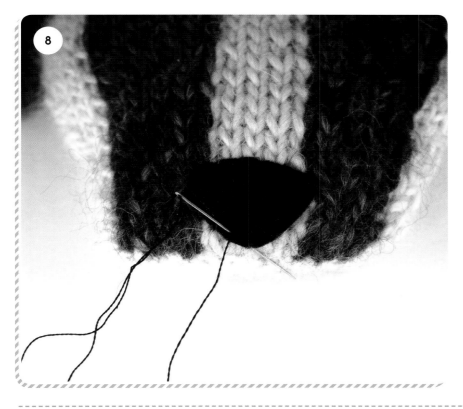

k1, kfb) in CC2, k4 in CC1, (kfb, k1, kfb) in CC2, (k1, kfb, k2, kfb, k8) in CC1. 38 sts

Row 7: (K9, kfb, k2, kfb, k2) in CC1, k5 in CC2, k4 in CC1, k5 in CC2, (k2, kfb, k2, kfb, k9) in CC1. 42 sts

Row 9: (K10, kfb, k2, kfb, k3) in CC1, (kfb, k3, kfb) in CC2, k4 in CC1, (kfb, k3, kfb) in CC2, (k3, kfb, k2, kfb, k10) in CC1. 50 sts

Rows 10–14: Work in pattern in stockinette st.

Row 15: (K10, k2tog, k2, ssk, k3) in CC1, k7 in CC2, k4 in CC1, k7 in CC2, (k3, k2tog, k2, ssk, k10) in CC1. 46 sts

Row 17: (K9, k2tog, k2, ssk, k2) in CC1, (ssk, k3, k2tog) in CC2, k4 in CC1, (ssk, k3, k2tog) in CC2, (k2, k2tog, k2, ssk, k9) in CC1. 40 sts

Row 19: (K8, k2tog, k2, ssk, k1) in CC1, k5 in CC2, k4 in CC1, k5 in CC2, (k1, k2tog, k2, ssk, k8) in CC1. 36 sts

Row 21: (K7, k2tog, k2, ssk) in CC1, (ssk, k1, k2tog) in CC2, k4 in CC1, (ssk, k1, k2tog) in CC2, (k2tog, k2, ssk, k7) in CC1. 30 sts

Rows 22–23: Work in pattern. Bind off using CC1.

Using a strand of CC1, seam up the back of the center of the head. (See figure 5.) Use CC1 to lightly sew across the neck. Stuff head very lightly. Use CC1 to seam up the snout. (See figure 6.)

Ears (make 2)
Using CC2, CO4.
Row 1: K1, kfb twice, k1. 6 sts

Row 2 and all even rows: Purl.
Row 3: K1, kfb, k2, kfb, k1. 8 sts
Row 5: K1, ssk, k2, k2tog, k1. 6 sts
Row 7: K1, ssk, k2tog, k1. 4 sts
Switch to CC1.
Row 8: Purl.
Row 9: Ssk, k2tog. Break yarn, pull tail through remaining sts. Weave end into purl side of ear.

Sew ears to top of head, centering on stripes. (See figure 7.)

Cut small oval from black felt. Use black thread to sew to front of snout. (See figure 8.)

Use CC1 to sew Xs for eyes. (See figure 9.)

Weave in all loose ends. Block scarf well.

Save the Yeti Scarf

With the threat of global warming looming, we've been hearing a lot about the plight of some of our most beloved arctic animals. Polar bears, for instance, have been getting a lot of attention. But there's one snow-loving creature that no one seems concerned for.

Where will the yeti go when the snow is gone? Will they be driven towards manmade cold environments in search of comfort? Will we find yeti seeking refuge in our ice skating rinks and meat lockers? I certainly hope not. In a heartfelt attempt to bring attention to this potential problem, I give you the Save the Yeti scarf. This scarf is knitted lengthwise. I love knitting scarves this way. They seem to knit up much faster for some reason. The yeti themselves are formed by a simple series of cables. So why not wrap your neck in a string of warm yeti and enjoy the snow, while you still can?

Materials

- 2 skeins Cascade Pacific Chunky in 01 white
- US size 10 (6.0 mm) 36 in. circular needle
- Cable needle
- Pack of tiny black buttons

Finished length:
70 inches (length can be adjusted by adding or subtracting 16 sts for each yeti repeat)

Gauge:
14 sts and 18 rows over 4 in. in stockinette st.

Glossary of abbreviations

CC – contrasting color
CO – cast on
cross 2 L – place 2 sts on cable
    needle, hold sts forward, knit
    next 2 sts, knit 2 sts from needle
cross 2 R – place 2 sts on cable
    needle, hold sts back, knit next
    2 sts, knit 2 sts from needle
k – knit
MC – main color
p – purl
st[s] – stitch[es]

Scarf

Knit length-wise:

CO276 sts. Work flat.

Rows 1–2: Knit.

Row 3: K2, (p4, k3, p2, k3, p4) 17 times, k2.

Rows 4: K2, (k4, p3, k2, p3, k4) 17 times, k2.

Rows 5–6: Repeat rows 3–4.

Row 7: K2, (p2, k1, cross 2 R, k2, cross 2 L, k1, p2) 17 times, k2 (see figure 1).

Row 8: K2, (k2, p12, k2) 17 times, k2.

Row 9: K2, (p2, k12, p2) 17 times, k2.

Row 10: K2, (k2, p12, k2) 17 times, k2.

Rows 11–12: Repeat rows 9–10.

Row 13: K2, (p4, cross 2 L, cross 2 R, p4) 17 times, k2.

Row 14: K2, (k4, p8, k4) 17 times, k2.

Row 15: K2, (p4, k8, p4) 17 times, k2.

Row 16: K2, (k4, p8, k4) 17 times, k2.

Row 17: K2, (p4, cross 2 R, cross 2 L, p4) 17 times, k2.

Row 18–19: Knit.

Bind off. Weave in loose ends. Block scarf. Sew buttons onto face for eyes (see figure 2).

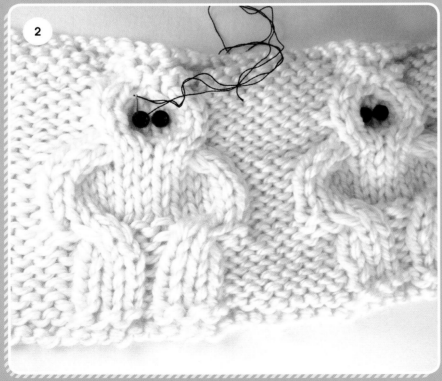

Robot Love Scarf

"Can robots fall in love?" This is the question my daughter asked me not long ago. I pictured happy beaming robots in love, holding hands, their mechanical hearts beating fast. So I turned the question back to her. "What do you think?"

"Maybe", she replied, "but I bet it would be noisy when they try to hug each other".

I then imagined cold metal robots trying to share an embrace, and the horrendous metal on metal noise that would make. Fortunately, the robot love scarf is both soft and warm, and feels much more pleasant than a robot hug. It is double knit, so the fabric is thick and reversible too.

Materials

- 2 skeins Cascade 220 wool in 9484 blue (MC)
- 2 skeins Cascade 220 wool in 8393 black (CC)
- US size 7 (4.5 mm) straight needles
- Yarn needle

Finished length:
65 in.

Gauge:
18 sts and 22 rows
over 4 in. in double
knitted stockinette stitch

Glossary of abbreviations

CC – contrasting color
CO – cast on
k – knit
MC – main color
p – purl
pm – place marker
st[s] – stitch[es]

Double Knitting

Double knitting is a simple technique for creating a reversible and thick fabric, appropriate for winter gear. My favorite characteristic of double knitting is the fact that stockinette lays flat. To work this technique, you will knit both sides of the scarf at once.

To work the chart in double knitting, on the odd numbered rows, you will first knit the color on the chart, and then purl the next st in the contrasting color. When knitting, bring both strands to the back of the fabric, and when purling, pull both strands to the front of the fabric. On the even numbered row, you do the reverse, knitting in the contrasting color, and then purling in the chart color. This may seem tedious at first, but I found that with a little practice, I could hold both colors at once, continental style, and move rather quickly. On the edges of the scarf, be sure to twist the strands together to prevent holes (see figure 1).

Scarf

CO52 in MC.

Row 1: (K1 in MC, p1 in CC) 26 times (see figure 2).

Row 2: (K1 in CC, p1 in CC) 26 times.

Begin chart. Repeat chart 11 times, or until scarf is desired length.

Bind off in MC. Weave in loose ends. Block.

1

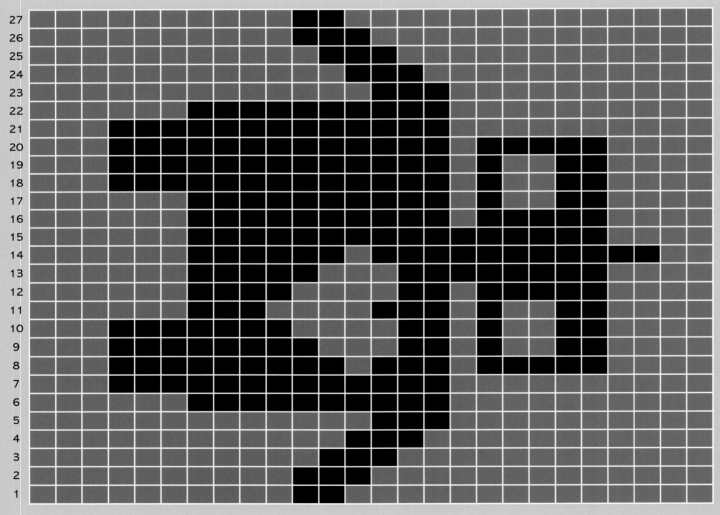

Knitting chart

Body Knitwits

Barnyard Buddies
Grump Sweater
Baby Bird Dress
Food Chain Sweater

Barnyard Buddies

When you think about it, babies have a lot in common with barn animals. They're messy, sometimes smelly, and they poop a lot. Though to be fair, babies are much cuter than your average cow. They'll be especially cute in this sweater, which features a barn door pocket for toting around their very own tiny barnyard friends. The sweater is knit in the round with raglan sleeves and a generous neck opening for your little piglet's big noggin.

Materials

- 5 skeins Cascade Luna in 741 dark orange (MC)
- 1 skein Cascade Luna in 738 white (CC)
- 1 skein Cascade 220 Superwash Sport in 1940 (pink for pig)
- 1 skein Cascade 220 Superwash Sport in 871 (white for cow)
- 1 skein Cascade 220 Superwash Sport in 821 (yellow for chicken)
- Scrap of orange yarn (for chicken legs)
- US size 7 (4.5 mm) 18 in. circular needle
- US size 6 (4.0 mm) 18 in. circular needle
- US size 7 (4.5 mm) double pointed needles
- US size 6 (4.0 mm) double pointed needles
- US size 3 (3.25 mm) double pointed needles
- Yarn needle
- Embroidery needle
- Stitch markers
- Toy stuffing
- Scraps of felt in pink, brown, and black
- 6 Tiny buttons for animal eyes
- Sewing thread to match felt

Finished size, chest circumference:
6 mths – 20 in.
12 mths – 21 in.
18 mths – 23 in.
24 mths – 24 in.

Gauge:
18 sts and 24 rows over
4 in. in stockinette st using
larger circular needle and MC

Glossary of abbreviations

CC – contrasting color
CO – cast on
k – knit
k2tog – decrease by knitting
   two together
kfb – increase by knitting into front
   and back of stitch
MC – main color
p – purl
p2tog – decrease by purling
   two together
pm – place marker
ssk – decrease by slip one, slip one,
   knit slipped stitches together
st[s] – stitch[es]

Body

Using US size 7 (4.5 mm) circular needle and MC, cast on 88 [92, 100, 108] stitches. Pm, join into the round. Switch to US size 6 (4.0 mm) circular needle.
Round 1: (K2, p2) to end.
Repeat round 1 for 5 [6, 7, 8] more rounds.
Switch back to US size 7 (4.5 mm) circular needle and knit even for 5¾ [6¾, 7½, 8¼] in.

Slip first 7 [7, 8, 8] sts on to scrap yarn for underarm. Place remaining body sts onto additional scrap yarn.
Set aside.

Sleeves (make 2)

Using US size 7 (4.5 mm) double pointed needles and MC, CO24 [28, 28, 32] sts, pm, join to knit in the round. Switch to US size 6 (4.0 mm) double pointed needles.
Round 1: (K2, p2) to end.

Repeat round 1: 2 [3, 4, 5] more times.
Switch back to US size 7 (4.5 mm) needles.
Knit even for 4 [7, 7, 7] rounds.
Next round: K1, kfb, k20 [24, 24, 28], kfb, k1. 26 [30, 30, 34] sts
Continue increasing 2 sts on each side of marker every 4 [7, 7, 7] rounds 2 [1, 3, 3] more times. 30 [32, 36, 40] sts
Work even until sleeve measures 5 [6½, 7, 8] in.

Slip the first 4 sts onto a piece of scrap yarn, k23 [25, 28, 32], place remaining sts on same scrap yarn.

Connect sleeves to body. Switch to double pointed needles when needed. Using US size 7 (4.5 mm) circular needle and MC, knit 23 [25, 28, 32] from first sleeve, pm, knit 37 [39, 42, 46] body sts, pm, place next 7 [7, 8, 8] sts on scrap yarn, knit 23 [25, 28, 32] from second sleeve, pm, knit 37 [39, 42, 46] body sts, place marker of different color to mark the beginning of the round. 120 [128, 140, 156] sts

Round 1: (K1, ssk, knit to 3 sts before next marker, k2tog, k1) 4 times. 112 [120, 132, 148] sts

Round 2: Knit.

Round 3: (K1, ssk, knit to 3 sts before next marker, k2tog, k1) 4 times. 104 [112, 124, 140] sts

Round 4: Purl.

Repeat rounds 1–4 three more times.

Repeat rounds 1–2 until 40 [48, 52, 60] sts remain.

Switch to US size 6 (4.0 mm) circular needle.

Next round: (K2, p2) to end.

Repeat this round 2 [2, 3, 3] more times. Switch to larger needle. Bind off loosely in pattern.

Place sets of underarm sts on 2 double pointed needles. Seam together using kitchener stitch (see figure 1).

Barn door pocket

Using US size 7 (4.5 mm) double pointed needles and CC, CO25.

Follow chart for pocket, twisting sts when changing colors to prevent holes.

Weave in all loose end. Block pieces well. Seam pocket to front of sweater along top and bottom (see figure 2).

Animals
Pig body

Using US size 3 (3.25 mm) double pointed needles and pink yarn, CO6, pm, join to knit in the round.

RRound 1: Kfb 6 times. 12 sts

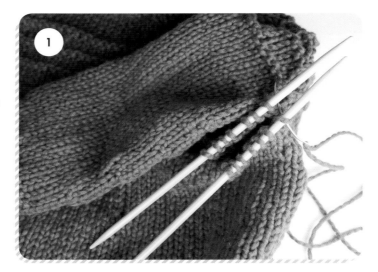

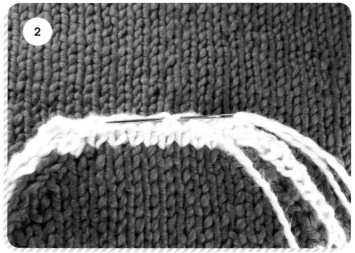

Round 2: (K1, kfb, k2, kfb, k1) twice. 16 sts
Round 3: (K1, kfb, k4, kfb, k1) twice. 20 sts
Round 4: Knit.
Round 5: (K1, kfb, k6 kfb, k1) twice. 24 sts
Knit 10 rounds.
Next round: (K1, k2tog, k6, k2tog, k1) twice. 20 sts
Knit 1 round. Stuff body. Divide for legs as follows:
K5, place the next 10 sts on a piece of scrap yarn, k5 (see figure 3). 10 sts
Knit 2 rounds even.
Next round: K2tog 5 times. Break yarn, pull tail through remaining sts. Knot, pull to inside of fabric.
Place 10 sts from scrap yarn on 2 double pointed needles. Complete same as for first leg.

Pig arms (make 2)
Using US size 3 (3.25 mm) double pointed needle and pink yarn, CO3. Knit an i-cord for ½ in.

Pig ears (make 2)
Using US size 3 (3.25 mm) double pointed needles and pink yarn, CO5.
Row 1: Knit.
Row 2: Purl.
Row 3: K2otg, k1, k2tog. 3 sts
Row 4: Purl.
Break yarn, pull tail through remaining sts, weave tail into purl side of ear.

Cow body
Using US size 3 (3.25 mm) double pointed needles and white yarn, CO6, pm, join to knit in the round.
Round 1: Kfb 6 times. 12 sts
Round 2: (K1, kfb, k2, kfb, k1) twice. 16 sts
Round 3: (K1, kfb, k4, kfb, k1) twice. 20 sts
Knit 14 rounds.
Next round: (K1, k2tog, k4, k2tog, k1) twice. 16 sts
Knit 1 round. Stuff body. Divide for legs as follows:
K4, place the next 8 sts on a piece of scrap yarn, k4. 8 sts

Knit 3 rounds even.
Next round: K2tog 4 times. Break yarn, pull tail through remaining sts. Knot, pull to inside of fabric.
Place 8 sts from scrap yarn on 2 double pointed needles. Complete same as for first leg.

Cow arms (make 2)
Complete same as for pig arms.

Chicken body
Using US size 3 (3.25 mm) double pointed needles and yellow yarn, CO6, pm, join to knit in the round.
Round 1: Kfb 6 times. 12 sts
Round 2: (K1, kfb, k2, kfb, k1) twice. 16 sts
Round 3: (K1, kfb, k4, kfb, k1) twice. 20 sts
Round 4: Knit.
Round 5: (K1, kfb, k6 kfb, k1) twice. 24 sts
Round 6: Knit.
Round 7: (K1, kfb, k8, kfb, k1) twice. 28 sts

Knit 8 rounds.
Next round: (K1, k2tog, k8, k2tog, k1) twice. 24 sts
Next round: (K1, k2tog, k6, k2tog, k1) twice. 20 sts
Next round: (K1, k2tog, k4, k2tog, k1) twice. 16 sts
Next round: (K1, k2tog, k2, k2tog, k1) twice. 12 sts
Next round: (K1, k2tog, twice, k1)

twice. 6 sts
Break yarn, pull tail through remaining sts.
Knot, pull to inside of fabric.

Chicken wings (make 2)
Using US size 3 (3.25 mm) double pointed needles and yellow yarn, CO7.
Row 1: Knit.
Row 2: Purl.
Row 3: K2tog, k3, k2tog. 5 sts

Row 4: Purl.
Row 5: K2otg, k1, k2tog. 3 sts
Row 6: Purl.
Break yarn, pull tail through remaining sts, weave tail into purl side of wing.

Chicken legs (make 2)
Complete same as for pig arms using orange yarn.

Assembling Animals

Seam arms, ears, and wings to bodies (see figure 4).
Cut felt pieces using template.
Seam pieces to animals using matching thread (see figure 5).
Sew buttons for eyes.
Sew French knots for nostrils.

Chicken

Pig

Cow

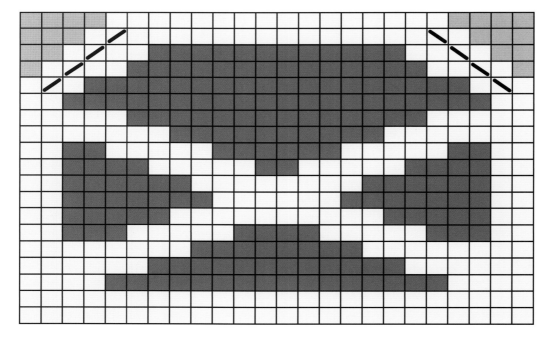

 K2tog on right side, p2tog on wrong side

 Ssk on right side, p2tog on wrong side

Knitting chart

Grump Sweater

I've found some toddlers are not fond of wearing hand knitted sweaters. In fact, I'm certain I've wrestled more than a few into submission. Spending endless hours knitting an article will sometimes give you superhuman strength when it comes times to dressing your child. But when you adorn your knits with funny monsters, the task to convince your child to wear it is often much easier. As you can see from the expression on the grumpy little monster's face, he's not fond of wearing sweaters either.

Materials

- 2 skeins Cascade Pacific in 30 gray (MC)
- 1 skein Cascade Pacific in 39 blue (CC1)
- 1 skein Cascade Pacific in 25 orange (CC2)
- 1 skein Cascade Pacific in 48 black (CC3)
- 1 skein Cascade Pacific in 02 white (CC4)
- US size 7 (4.5 mm) straight needles
- US size 7 (4.5 mm) double pointed needles
- Yarn needle
- Stitch markers

Finished size (actual measurements):

	Length	Chest circumference
1-2 yrs	13 in.	24 in.
3-4 yrs	14 in.	26 in.
4-5 yrs	15 in.	28 in.

Gauge:
20 sts and 24 rows over 4 in. in stockinette st

Glossary of abbreviations

BO – bind off
CC – contrasting color
CO – cast on
k – knit
k2tog – decrease by knitting two together
kfb – increase by knitting into front and back of stitch
MC – main color
p – purl
p2tog – decrease by purling two together
pm – place marker
ssk – decrease by slip one, slip one, knit slipped stitches together
st[s] – stitch[es]

Back

Using straight needles and MC, CO 60 (64, 70) begin knitting flat.
Row 1: (K2, p2) to end.
Row 2: (K2, p2) to end.
Repeat these 2 rows until piece measures 1½ (1¾, 2) in. from edge.
Next row: Knit.
Next row: Purl.
Continue in stockinette st until the piece measures 8 (9, 10) in. from edge, ending with a purl row. Begin shaping armholes.
Next row: BO4, knit to end. 56 (60, 66) sts
Next row: BO4, purl to end. 54 (58, 64) sts
Work 2 rows in stockinette.
Next row: K1, k2tog, k48 (52, 58), ssk, k1. 52 (56, 62) sts
Decrease in this manner 2 sts every

2 rows 12 times. 26 (30, 32) sts

Begin shaping neckline

Next row: K1, k2tog, k5 (6, 6), BO10 (12, 14), k5 (6, 6), ssk, k1. 14 (16, 16) sts
Next row: P4 (5, 5), p2tog, p1, turn, continue knitting left side.
Next row: K1, k2tog (k3tog, k3tog,), ssk, k1.
Next row: P2tog twice.
Break yarn, pull tail through remaining st.
Reconnect yarn to remaining sts, beginning with a purl row:
Next row: P1, p2tog, p4 (5, 5).
Next row: K1, k2tog (k3tog, k3tog), ssk, k1.
Next row: P2tog twice. Break yarn, pull tail through remaining st.

Front

Cast on and begin knitting same as for back. When piece measures 3½ (4, 5) in. place markers for chart placement: P16 (18, 21), pm, p28, pm, p16 (18, 21). Begin chart, starting with a knit row. Knit remaining piece as for back, completing chart between markers.

Sleeves (make 2)

Using double pointed needles and MC, CO28 (30, 32), pm, join to knit in the round.
Round 1: (K2, p2) to end.
Repeat first round 5 more times.
Rounds 7–11: Knit.
Round 12: K1, kfb, k24, (26, 28), kfb, k1. 30 (32, 34) sts
Continue increasing in this manner 2 sts

every 6th round 8 more times.
Knit even until piece measures 11 (11½, 12) in. 46 (48, 50) sts

Begin shaping for armhole
Next round: K42 (44, 46), BO4. 42 (44, 46) sts
Next round: BO4, k38 (40, 42). 38 (40, 42) sts
Turn and begin knitting straight.
Next row: Purl.
Next row: K1, k2tog, k32 (34, 36), ssk, k1. 36 (38, 40) sts
Continue decreasing in this manner 2 sts every other row 12 (12, 13) times. 12 (14, 14) sts
Bind off.

Assembly

Weave in loose ends.
Block all pieces. Seam together front and back at lower edge (see figure 1). Seam sleeves to front and back, beginning at upper edge, and matching flat edge under arms (see figure 2).

Neckline
Using double pointed needles and beginning at center back, pick up 68 sts evenly around edge of neck, 17 sts on each needle. Pm, join to knit in the round (see figure 3).

Round 1: (K2, p2) to marker. Repeat round 1 three more times.
Bind off in pattern very loosely. Weave in loose ends.

Note: When completing chart, wind all contrasting colors into bobbins.
Twist sts together when changing colors to prevent holes.

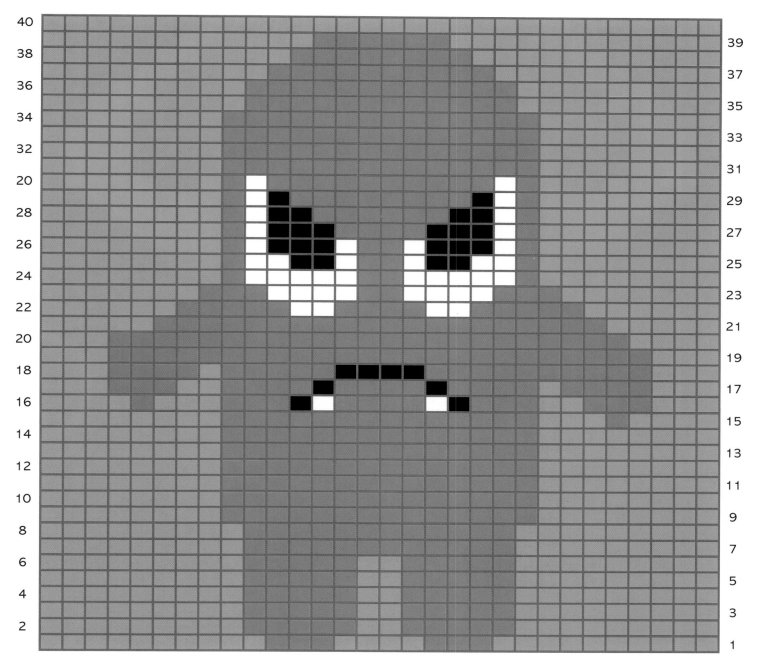

Knitting chart

Baby Bird Dress

I always loved knitting dresses for my daughter to wear in the spring. It's finally warm enough to bare the knees. The yard is full of flowers and overrun with birds. She'll spend hours exploring, reporting back every new plant that has newly sprouted from the ground as well as a list of every spotted bird or insect. Ultra Pima is the perfect yarn for such an occasion. The colors are beautiful, and the fabric has a nice drape, and is completely machine washable.

Materials

- 2 [2, 3, 3] skeins Cascade Ultra Pima in 3703 magenta (MC)
- 1 skein Cascade Ultra Pima in 3776 pale pink (CC)
- US size 5 (3.75 mm) circular needle 16in.
- US size 5 (3.75 mm) double pointed needles
- Stitch markers
- Yarn needle

Finished chest circumference:
6 mths – 18 in.
12 mths – 19 in.
18 mths – 21 in.
24 mths – 22 in.

Gauge:
20 sts and 26 rows over 4in. in stockinette st

Glossary of abbreviations

CC – contrasting color
CO – cast on
k – knit
k2tog – decrease by knitting two together
MC – main color
p – purl
pm – place marker
ssk – decrease by slip one, slip one, knit slipped stitches together
st[s] – stitch[es]
yo – yarn over needle

Using circular needle and MC, CO155 [160,198, 204] sts, pm, join to knit in the round. Be careful not to twist sts.
Rounds 1–2: Knit.
Round 3: (K2tog, yo) to end.
Rounds 4–5: Knit.
Complete scallop edge:
Round 6: Pick up first st from cast on edge under first st on needle. Place the st on the needle so that the knit side faces, and knit together with first stitch. Continue with all remaining sts.
Rounds 7–9: Knit.
Round 10: (K0 [1, 2, 3], knit first row from chart) 5 [5, 6, 6] times.
Repeat last round until chart is completed.
Knit even until skirt measures 9 [10, 12, 14] inches from cast on edge.

Gather waist
Size 6 mths: Next round: K2tog 77 times, k1. 78 sts.

Size 12 mths: Next round: K2tog to end. 80 sts
Size 18 mths: Next round: (K2tog, k1) to end. 132 sts
Knit 4 rounds.
Next round: (K2tog, k1) to end. 88 sts
Size 24 mths: Next round: (K2tog, k1) to end. 136 sts
Knit 4 rounds.
Next round: K3, (k2tog, k1) 86 times, k3, k2tog. 92 sts

Bodice
All sizes: Knit even until dress measures 13 [14, 16, 18] in.

Begin dividing for sleeves
Place the first 4 [4, 5, 5] sts on a piece of scrap yarn for underarm. Place the next 35 [36, 39, 41] sts on another scrap of yarn for the front. Repeat between (*) for other underarm and back. Put aside and begin sleeves.

Sleeves (make 2)
Using double pointed needles and MC, CO28 [30, 32, 34], pm, join to knit in the round.
Rounds 1–2: Knit.
Round 3: (K2tog, yo) to end.
Rounds 4–5: Knit.

Complete scallop edge
Round 6: Pick up first st from cast on edge under first st on needle. Place the st on the needle so that the knit side faces, and knit together with first stitch. Continue with all remaining sts.
Round 7: Knit.
Round 8: K24 [26, 27, 29], place the remaining 4 [4, 5, 5] sts on a piece of scrap yarn for underarm.

Connect sleeves to body
From the first sleeve k24 [26, 27, 29], pm, k35 [36, 39, 41] sts for the front, pm, k24 [26, 27, 29] from the second

sleeve, pm, k35 [36, 39, 41] sts for the back, place a different colored marker to mark beginning of round (see figure 1). 118 [124, 132, 140] sts

Round 1: Knit.

Round 2: (K1, k2tog, knit to 3 sts before nest marker, ssk, k1) 4 times. 114 [120, 128, 136] sts

Repeat rounds 1–2 until 54 [60 , 64, 72] sts remain.

Next round: (K1, p1) around.

Bind off loosely.

Place sts from underarm on 2 double pointed needles. Use kitchener stitch to close up hole (see figure 2).

Weave in loose ends. Block dress well

Place sts from underarm on 2 double pointed needles. Use Kitchner stitch to close up hole. (see figure 2)

Weave in loose ends. Block dress well.

1

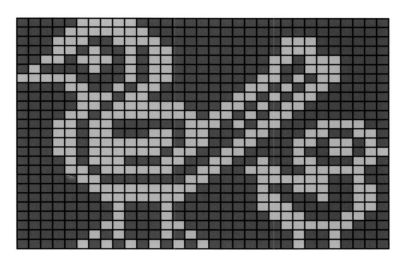

Knitting chart

Food Chain Sweater

Circular yoke sweaters are my very favorite kind of sweater to knit. I find the fit works really well for children and adults alike. The ease in the chest makes fitting less of a hassle, and there are no sleeves to set. Designing Fair Isle yoke charts can be really fun. I knew I wanted to have an aquatic theme, so I asked Sophia what sea animal I should use, and she immediately responded "sharks", which surprised me. I thought for sure she'd pick something cuter and less terrifying, but I suppose sharks are quite popular. They even have their own week on TV, and as the saying goes, "Live every week like it's shark week".

Materials

- 3 skeins Cascade Pacific in 64 blue-gray (MC)
- 1 skein Cascade Pacific in 33 green (CC1)
- 1 skein Cascade Pacific in 02 white (CC2)
- 1 skein Cascade Pacific in 34 gray (CC3)
- 1 skein Cascade Pacific in 39 bright blue (CC4)
- US size 7 (4.5 mm) circular needle 16 in.
- US size 7 (4.5 mm) double pointed needles
- US size 6 (4.0 mm) circular needle 16 in.
- US size 6 (4.0 mm) double pointed needles
- Stitch marker
- Yarn needle
- 1 pack of very small blue buttons

Finished size (actual measurements):

	Length	Chest circumference
4 yrs	16 in.	26 in.
6 yrs	17 in.	28 in.
8 yrs	19 in.	30 in.
10 yrs	22 in.	32 in.

Gauge:
20 sts and 24 rows over 4 in. in stockinette st using larger needles

Glossary of abbreviations

BO – bind off
CC – contrasting color
CO – cast on
k – knit
k2tog – decrease by knitting two together
kfb – increase by knitting into front and back of stitch
MC – main color
p – purl
pm – place marker
st[s] – stitch[es]
w&t – wrap and turn

Body

Using US size 7 (4.5 mm) circular needle and MC, CO128 [140, 148, 160], pm, join to knit in the round.
Switch to US size 6 (4.0 mm) circular needle.
Round 1: (K2, p2) to end.
Repeat round 1 until edge measures 1¼ [1½, 1¾, 2] in.
Switch to US size 7 (4.5 mm) needle.
Knit even until piece measures 9½ [10½, 12, 13½] in.
Next round: (BO8, k56 [62, 66, 72]) twice.

Place remaining sts on scrap yarn and set aside.

Sleeves (make 2)

Using US size 7 (4.5 mm) double pointed needles, CO32 [32, 36, 40].
Switch to US size 6 (4.0 mm) needles.
Round 1: (K2, p2) to end.
Repeat round 1 until piece measures ¾ [1, 1¼, 1½] in.
Switch to US size 7 (4.5 mm) needles.
Rounds 1–5: Knit.
Round 6: K1, kfb, k28 [28, 32, 36], kfb, k1. 34 [34, 38, 42] sts

Continue increasing 2 sts in this manner every 6th round 7 [9, 8, 8] times.
48 [52, 54, 58] sts
Continue knitting even until piece measures 11 [11½, 13, 14] in.
Next round: BO4, k40 [44, 46, 50], BO4.
40 [44, 46, 50] sts
Place sts on scrap yarn. Set aside.
Combine body and sleeves for yoke.
Switch back to double pointed needles when stitches become too tight.
Using US size 7 (4.5 mm) circular needle and MC, pick up and knit 40 [44, 46, 50] sts from first sleeve, then 56 [62, 66, 72]

sts from front of sweater, sts from second sleeve, and remaining sts from back of sweater. Pm, join to knit in the round. 192 [212, 224, 244] sts

Round 1: Knit, decreasing 2 [2, 4, 4] sts evenly around. 190 [210, 220, 240] sts

Rounds 2–14: Begin chart 1. Repeat 19 [21, 22, 24] times around yoke.

Switch back to MC. Knit even until yoke measures 2½ [2¾, 3, 3] in.

Next round: (K2tog, k3) to end. 152 [168, 176, 192] sts

Begin chart 2. Repeat 19 [21, 22, 24] times around yoke.

Switch back to MC. Knit even until yoke measures 3¾ [4¼, 4¾, 5] in.

Next round: (K2tog, k2) to end. 114 [126, 132, 144] sts

Knit even until yoke measures 5 [5¾, 6¼, 6¼] in.

Next round: (K2tog, k1) to end. 76 [84, 88, 96] sts.

Knit until yoke measures 6¼ [7¼, 7¾, 8¼] in.

Shape neckline with short rows as follows:

Next row: W&t, p22 [24, 26, 28].

Next row: W&t, k17 [19, 21, 23].

Next row: W&t, p12 [14, 16, 18].

Next row: W&t, knit to marker. Knit 1 round even.

Switch to US size 6 (4.0 mm) needles.

Next round: (K2, p2) to marker.

Repeat last round. Switch to US size 7 (4.5 mm) needles.

Bind off loosely in pattern.

Weave in loose ends.

Seam up armholes (see figure 1).

Sew buttons on as shark eyes (see figure 2).

Block sweater.

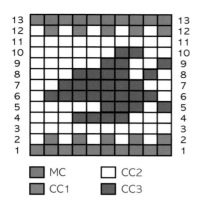

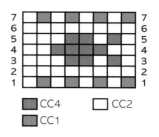

MC

CC1

CC2

CC3

CC4

CC1

CC2

Knitting charts

CAN YOU KNIT ME FURTHER AWAY PLEASE?!

Hand Knitwits

Lobster Claw Mittens

I often find it difficult to convince my kids to wear mittens when they play outside in the winter. But inevitably they return to the house complaining about numb fingers. Plain mittens are fine, but the kids seem a lot more enthusiastic to wear lobster claws while playing outside. I love knitting cords onto the mittens. I-cord isn't my favorite knitting task, but it's generally easier than digging through the snow to find your handiwork later on. So keep your little lobster's claws warm with this simple pattern. However, I have one disclaimer: Mothers beware. Putting claws on your child will most likely encourage them to pinch you.

Materials

- 1 skein Cascade Pacific in 36 red
- 1 set US size 7 (4.5 mm) double pointed needles
- 1 set US size 4 (3.5 mm) double pointed needles
- Yarn needle
- Stitch marker

Finished hand circumference:
Small, 2–4 yrs – 5½ in.
Medium, 4–6 yrs – 6 in.
Large, 6–8 yrs. – 6½ in.

Gauge:
20 sts and 24 rows over 4 in. in stockinette st. with US size 7 (4.5 mm) needles

Glossary of abbreviations

CO – cast on
k – knit
k2tog – decrease by knitting two together
kfb – increase by knitting into front and back of stitch
p – purl
pm – place marker
st[s] – stitch[es]

Cuff (make 2)
Using larger needles, CO28 [30, 32] sts. Pm, join to knit in the round.
Round 1: (K1, p1) to end.
Repeat round 1, 10 [11, 12] times.

Hand
Round 1: (Kfb, k13 [14, 15]) twice. 30 [32, 34] sts
Round 2: Knit.
Round 3: Kfb, k12 [13, 14], kfb, k2, kfb, k12 [13, 14], kfb. 34 [36, 38] sts
Rounds 4–5: Knit.
Round 6: K1, kfb, k13 [14, 15], kfb, k2, kfb, k13 [14, 15], kfb, k1. 38 [40, 42] sts
Rounds 7–8: Knit.
Round 9: K2, kfb, k14 [15, 16], kfb, k2, kfb, k14 [15, 16], kfb, k2. 42 [44, 46] sts
Rounds 10–12: Knit.
Round 13: K3, kfb, k34 [36, 38], kfb, k3. 44 [46, 48] sts

Size Small only
Knit 2 rounds. Skip to dividing for thumb gusset.

Sizes Medium and Large
Rounds 14–17: Knit.
Round 18: K4, kfb, k36 [38], kfb, k4. 48 [50] sts

Size Large only
Rounds 19–22: Knit.
Round 23: K5, kfb, k38, kfb, k5. 52 sts

All sizes
Begin dividing for thumb gusset:
Place the first 5 [6, 7] sts on a piece of scrap yarn. Reconnect working yarn to the next st.
Knit 34 [36, 38] sts. Place the last 5 [6, 7] sts of the scrap yarn. Begin working upper hand (see figure 1). 34 [36, 38] sts
Split sts evenly between 2 needles.
Round 1: K1, k2tog, 28 [30, 32], k2tog, k1. 32 [34, 36] sts
Round 2: Knit.
Round 3: K1, k2tog, 26 [28, 30], k2tog, k1. 30 [32, 34] sts
Knit 2 [4, 6] rounds even.
*Next round: K1, kfb, k10 [11, 12] k2tog, k2, k2tog, k10 [11, 12] kfb, k1.
Knit 1 round.
Repeat (*) round.
Continue increasing 2 sts on the thumb side of the hand every 2 [3, 4] rounds. Continue decreasing 2 sts on the outside of the hand every round until 20 [22, 24] sts remain. Cut yarn, leaving a long tail. Close opening at top of hand using the kitchener stitch (see figure 2).

Thumb
Place sts from scrap yarn on 2 needles, divided evenly. Attach yarn and begin working at inside of thumb.
10 [12, 14] sts
Round 1: Knit.

Round 2: K2tog, k1 [2, 3], kfb, k2, kfb, k1 [2, 3], k2tog.

Rounds 3–4: Repeat rounds 1 and 2.

Round 5: Knit.

Round 6: Kfb, k1 [2, 3], k2tog, k2, k2tog, k1 [2, 3], kfb.

Round 7: K3 [4, 5], k2tog twice, k3 [4, 5]. 8 [10, 12] sts

Round 8: Knit.

Continue decreasing 2 sts on outer edge of thumb every other round until 6 sts remain.

Break yarn, draw through remaining sts, knot, weave loose end into wrong side of fabric.

Claw ridges

Thumb ridge

*Using smaller needles, CO1. Knit flat.

Row 1: Kfb. 2 sts

Row 2: Kfb, k1. 3 sts

Row 3: K2, kfb. 4 sts

Row 4: Knit.

Row 5: K2, k2tog. 3 sts

Row 6: K2tog, k1. 2 sts

Row 7: K2tog. 1 st*

Break yarn. Pull tail through remaining st.

Hand ridge

Complete same as for small ridge, repeating between *s three times.

Press ridges lightly. Beginning at top edge, sew long ridge onto side of hand (see figure 3). Sew small ridge onto top inside edge of thumb.

Cord (optional)

At outer edge of cuff, use a larger size double pointed needle, pick up and knit 3 stitches from cuff. Knit an i-cord for 3 [4, 5] feet. Attach other end to other cuff (see figure 4).

Cyclops Friends Mittens

When I was little, I loved making strings of paper dolls. Although I would often pass on the standard girl in a dress shape in favor of something more interesting. I thought of this while designing the Cyclops Friends Mittens, a string of happy little monsters, wrapping around my daughter's mittens. This is a fairly simple Fair Isle pattern, knitted stranded and in the round. It's a good introduction to Fair Isle if you've been itching to try it yourself.

Materials

- 1 1 skein Cascade 220 Superwash in Cream (MC)
- 1 skein Cascade 220 Superwash in Red (CC1)
- 1 skein Cascade 220 Superwash in Blue (CC2)
- 1 Skein Cascade 220 Superwash in Beige (CC3)
- 1 set US size 6 (4.0 mm) double pointed needles
- Stitch marker
- 1 pack of tiny black buttons
- Yarn needle

Finished hand circumference:
Toddler (Child, Women, Men)
5½ (6¾, 8, 9¼) in.

Gauge:
24 sts and 30 rows
over 4" in stockinette st

Glossary of abbreviations

CC – contrasting color
k – knit
k2tog – decrease by knitting
  two together
kfb – increase by knitting into front
  and back of stitch
M1L – make 1 left slanted, take
  the left-hand needle and pick
  up the bar between the stitches
  from front to back. Use the right
  needle to knit this bar through
  the back of the loop.
M1R – make 1 right slanted, take
  the left-hand needle and pick
  up the bar between the stitches
  from front to back. Use the right
  needle to knit this bar through
  the front of the loop.
MC – main color
p – purl
pm – place marker
st[s] – stitch[es]

Cuff

With MC cast on 32 (40, 48, 56) sts.
Pm, join to knit in the round.
Work k1, p1 ribbing until cuff measures
1¾ (2½, 2¾, 3) in.

Hand

Begin stockinette st, and increase 1 st at end of round. 33 (41, 49, 57) sts
Shape thumb gusset:
Knit across 16 (20, 24, 28) sts, pm, M1L, k1, M1R, pm, knit to end. 35 (43, 51, 59) sts
Knit 2 rounds even.
Knit to marker, M1L, knit to marker, M1R, knit to end. 37 (45, 53, 61) sts
Increase 2 sts inside gusset markers every 3 rounds 3 (3, 5, 5) more times. 43 (51, 63, 71) sts
Knit 1 round even.
Add CC3, k1 in CC3, k1 in MC. Continue to alternate to end of round.
Cut CC3. Switch to CC2. Knit to marker,

M1L, knit to 2nd marker, M1R, knit to end.
Cut CC2. Switch to MC.
Knit to marker. Place sts between markers onto a piece of scrap yarn, remove markers, knit to end of round
(see figure 1). 32 (40, 48, 56) sts
Knit 1 (1, 3, 4) rounds even.

Hand

Make bobbins in both MC and CC1.
Begin chart, repeating 4 (5, 6, 7) times each round.
Run both colors loosely along inside of mitten, being careful to twist when changing colors to avoid making a hole.
Knit 1 (1, 3, 4) rounds even.
Switch to CC2. Knit 1 round.
Add CC3, k1 in CC3, k1 in MC. Continue to alternate to end of round.

Shape top

Switch back to MC.
Round 1: Knit around, decreasing 2 (4, 0,

2) sts evenly. 30 (36, 48, 54) sts
Round 2 and all remaining even rounds:
Knit.
Toddler size: skip to round 11.
Child's size: skip to round 9.
Women's size: skip to round 5.
Men's size only: Round 3: (K2tog, k7) 6 times. 48 sts
Round 5: (K2tog, k6) 6 times. 42 sts
Round 7: (K2tog, k5) 6 times. 36 sts
Round 9: (K2tog, k4) 6 times. 30 sts
Round 11: (K2tog, k3) 6 times. 24 sts
Round 13: (K2tog, k2) 6 times. 18 sts

Round 15: (K2tog, k1) 6 times. 12 sts
Round 17: K2tog 6 times. 6 sts
Break yarn, pull tail through remaining sts.
Knot and pull knot to inside of fabric.

Thumb

Divide sts from scrap yarn evenly onto
double pointed needles. Attach MC.
13 (13, 17, 17) sts

Sizes toddler and child:
Round 1: K7, kfb, k5, pick up a st from
gap inside of thumb and knit. 15 sts

Sizes women and men:
Round 1: (K5, kfb) twice, k5, pick up a st
from gap inside of thumb and knit. 20 sts

Continue for all sizes:
Knit 3 (4, 7, 10) rounds even.

Sizes women and men:
Next round: (K2tog, k2) 5 times. 15 sts

Continue for all sizes:
Next round: (K2tog, k1) 5 times. 10 sts
Next round: K2tog 5 times. 5 sts
Break yarn, pull tail through remaining sts.
Knot and pull knot to inside of fabric.
Turn mitten inside-out. Weave in all loose
ends. Block well. Sew tiny buttons onto
mittens as monster eyes.

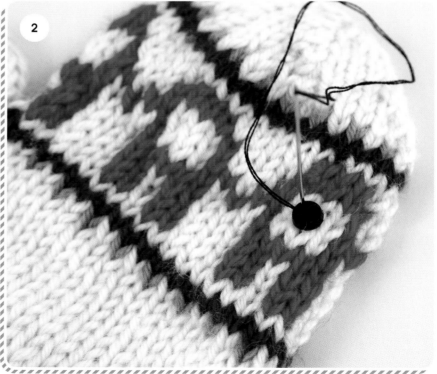

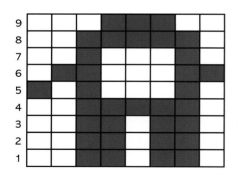

Knitting chart

Ninja Mitts

Ninjas get cold in winter just like everyone else, but it can be cumbersome throwing stars and climbing walls with gloves on. Fingerless ninja mitts are perfect for outdoor covert activities, such as secret knitting during my son's chilly late fall soccer games, or trying to feed quarters into a parking meter during a blizzard. The ninja mitts are a quick knit, and the Cherub DK yarn is incredibly soft. Ninjas don't like scratchy yarn any more than the rest of us.

Materials

- 1 skein Cascade Cherub DK in 40 black (MC)
- 1 skein Cascade Cherub DK in 01 white (CC1)
- 1 skein Cascade Cherub DK in 25 red (CC2)
- US size 3 (3.25 mm) double pointed needles
- Stitch markers
- Yarn needle

Finished size:
Women's one size, finished wrist circumference 7 in.

Gauge:
23 sts and 30 rows over 4 in. in stockinette st

Glossary of abbreviations

CC – contrasting color
CO – cast on
k – knit
m – make one by knitting the bar
   between stitches
MC – main color
p – purl
pm – place marker
st[s] – stitch[es]

Cuff
Using MC, CO48, pm, join to knit in the round.
Round 1: (K2, p2) 14 times.
Repeat round 1, 4 times.
Round 16: M1, k48. 49 sts
Rounds 17–21: Knit.
Begin creating thumb gusset.
Round 22: K48, pm, m1, k1, m1. 51 sts
Round 23: Knit.
Round 24: K48, m1, k3, m1. 53 sts
Round 25: Knit.
Continue increasing every other round, 1 st after first marker, and 1 st before second marker, until you have 17 sts between markers (see figure 1). 66 sts
Next round: K48. Place 17 sts between markers on a piece of scrap yarn (see figure 2). 48 sts
Next round: K48.
Switch to CC1. Work chart, repeating 8 times each round.

Tips for Fair Isle knitting
- Wind yarn into bobbins to prevent tangling (see figure 3).
- Twist yarn when changing colors between sts to prevent holes.
- Knit loosely, carrying all colors behind sts on inside of mitt. Pulling sts tight will make the mitts pucker.

Switch to MC to complete top of hand.
Next round: Knit.
Next round: (K2, p2) 8 times. Repeat this row twice more. Bind off in pattern.

Thumb
Using MC, pick up and knit 17 sts from scrap yarn, dividing between double pointed needles.
Pick up 1 sts from the inside of the thumb to prevent a hole from forming. 18 sts
Round 1: (K2, p2) 4 times, k2.
Repeat round 1 three more times. Bind off in pattern. Weave in loose ends. Block mitts.

1

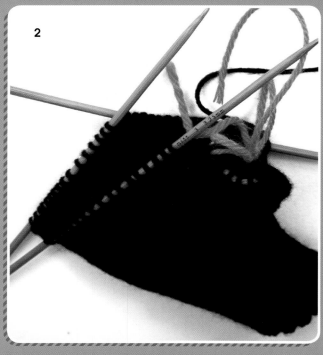

2

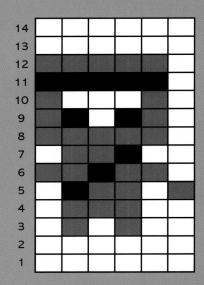

Knitting chart

BECAUSE NUMB HANDS AND NUNCHUKS DON'T MIX!

Accordion Handwarmer

Muffs, or handwarmers, went out of fashion long ago. I did have one made of fur when I was a kid. It was very cozy, though not very practical for a child who never sits still. Likewise, having a handwarmer that is shaped like a concertina may not seem like a very practical accessory, but it is an interesting way to keep your hands warm. So why wear an ordinary pair of mittens, when you could stuff your hands into a knitted squeezebox and hum a Zydeco tune?

Materials

- 1 skein Cascade Pacific in 40 blue (MC)
- 1 skein Cascade Pacific in 21 turquoise (CC)
- 1 set US size 7 (4.5 mm) double pointed needles
- Stitch marker
- Yarn needle
- Toy Stuffing

Finished size:
12 in.

Gauge:
18 sts and 24 rows over 4in. in stockinette st

Glossary of abbreviations

CC – contrasting color
CO – cast on
k – knit
k2tog – decrease by knitting
  two together
kfb – increase by knitting into front
  and back of stitch
MC – main color
p – purl
pm – place marker
ssk – decrease by slip one, slip one,
  knit slipped stitches together
st[s] – stitch[es]

Using MC, CO84, pm, join to knit in the round.
Round 1: (K1, p1) to end.
Round 2: (P1, k1) to end.
Round 3: (K1, p1) to end.
Rounds 4–9: Knit.
Round 10: Purl.
Rounds 11–12: Knit.
Round 13: Purl.
Switch to CC.
Round 14: Knit.
Round 15: (K2tog, k10, ssk) 6 times. 72 sts
Round 16: (K2tog, k8, ssk) 6 times. 60 sts
Round 17: (K2tog, k6, ssk) 6 times. 48 sts
Round 18: (K2tog, k4, ssk) 6 times. 36 sts
Round 19: (Kfb, k4, kfb) 6 times. 48 sts
Round 20: (Kfb, k6, kfb) 6 times. 60 sts
Round 21: (Kfb, k8, kfb) 6 times. 72 sts
Round 22: (Kfb, k10, kfb) 6 times. 84 sts
Round 23: Knit.
Repeat rounds 15–23 5 more times.
Knit 1 round.

Switch back to MC.
Next round: Purl.
Knit 2 rounds.
Purl 1 round.
Knit 6 rounds.
Next round: (K1, p1) to end.
Next round: (P1, k1) to end.
Next round: (K1, p1) to end.
Knit 1 round.
Continuing on same sts without breaking yarn, begin lining:
Round 1: (K1, k2tog, k8, ssk, k1) 6 times. 72 sts
Round 2: (K1, k2tog, k6, ssk, k1) 6 times. 60 sts
Round 3: (K1, k2tog, k4, ssk, k1) 6 times. 48 sts
Round 4: (K1, k2tog, k2, ssk, k1) 6 times. 36 sts
Continue knitting even for 11 inches from last decrease round. Bind off loosely, leaving a long tail for seaming.

Finishing

Using a warm iron with no steam, press accordion folds 1 layer at a time (see figure 1).
Turn lining and pull through center of folds. Stuff bottom end, pressing into shape (see figure 2).
Seam bound off edge off lining to cast on edge, stuffing top end of accordion as you go (see figure 3). Squeeze into shape.

3

Foot
Knitwits

Roller Skate Booties
Baby Elf Shoes
Raincloud Socks
Bug in a Rug Legwarmers
Bigfoot Slippers

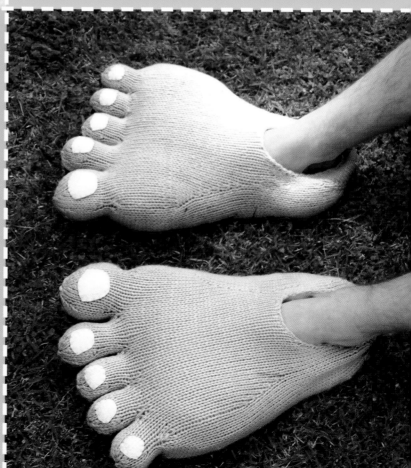

Roller Skate Booties

Two years ago, a group of very ambitious women in my hometown decided to form a roller derby team. Since I grew up in the rink and love roller skating, I eagerly joined, imagining all the adorable and sassy things I would knit to wear during bouts. For about two months, I endured the battering and bruising that comes along with roller derby training, until I realized that being a roller girl meant living with the constant and likely danger of serious injuries to my wrists and fingers. Also, it turned out I wasn't nearly as tough or talented a skater as I was in my own head. In fact, I'm a bit of a train wreck on wheels. So I gave it up for the sake of my knitting career, but continue to live in complete admiration of these incredibly cool, tough, and athletic women. With that in mind, I'm dedicating these roller booties to the roller girls of the future.

Materials

- 1 skein Cascade 220 in 9468 blue (MC)
- 1 skein Cascade 220 in 8505 white (CC1)
- 1 skein Cascade 220 in 8555 black (CC2)
- 1 set US size 6 (4.0 mm) double pointed needles
- Stitch marker
- Yarn needle
- Embroidery needle
- Scraps of felt in black and yellow
- Black thread
- Toy stuffing
- 8 yellow buttons: ½ in.

Finished size:
4 in. long

Gauge:
18 sts and 24 rows over
4 in. in stockinette st.

Glossary of abbreviations

CC – contrasting color
CO – cast on
k – knit
k2tog – decrease by knitting two together
kfb – increase by knitting into front and back of stitch
MC – main color
p – purl
pm – place marker
ssk – decrease by slip one, slip one, knit slipped stitches together
st[s] – stitch[es]
yo – yarn over needle

Sole (make 2)
Using CC1, CO5.
Row 1: K1, kfb, k1, kfb, k1. 7 sts
Row 2: Purl.
Row 3: K1, kfb, k3, kfb, k1. 9 sts
Rows 4–22: Work in stockinette st.
Row 23: K1, k2tog, k3, k2tog, k1. 7 sts
Bind off. Weave in loose ends.

Body (make 2)
Using CC1, pick up and purl 36 sts evenly around perimeter of sole. Pm, join to knit in the round (see figure 1). Switch to CC2.
Round 1: Knit.
Switch to CC1.
Round 2: K13, k2tog, k6, ssk, k13. 34 sts

Switch to MC.
Round 3: Knit.
Round 4: K12, k2tog, k6, ssk, k12. 32 sts
Round 5: K11, k2tog, k6, ssk, k11. 30 sts
Round 6: K10, k2tog, k6, ssk, k10. 28 sts

Divide for tongue
Break yarn. Place the first 15 sts on a piece of scrap yarn. Place the next 6 sts on 1 double pointed needle. Place the remaining 15 sts on a piece of scrap yarn. Continue working sts on needle as follows:
Reconnect MC to begin with a knit row.
Row 1: K1, kfb, k2, kfb, k1. 8 sts
Row 2: Purl.
Row 3: K1, kfb, k4, kfb, k1. 10 sts

Row 4: Purl.
Row 5: K1, kfb, k6, kfb, k1. 12 sts
Rows 6–9: Work in stockinette st.
Bind off.
Place 30 sts from scrap yarn on double pointed needles. Reconnect MC and begin with a knit row.
Row 1: Knit.
Row 2: Purl.
Row 3: K2tog, yo, k2tog, k14, k2tog, yo, k2tog. 28 sts
Row 4: Purl.
Row 5: Knit.
Row 6: Purl.
Row 7: K2tog, yo, k2tog, k12, k2tog, yo, k2tog. 26 sts
Bind off purlwise. Weave in loose ends.

Wheels (make 8)

Using CC2, CO6, pm, join to knit in the round.

Round 1: Kfb 6 times. 12 sts
Round 2: Kfb 12 times. 24 sts
Rounds 3–5: Knit.
Round 6: K2tog 12 times. 12 sts
Round 7: K2tog 6 times. 6 sts

Stuff wheel lightly, break yarn, pull tail through remaining sts, knot, pull knot to inside of wheel. Press wheel into shape.

Toe stops (make 2)

Using CC2, CO6, pm, join to knit in the round.

Round 1: Kfb 6 times. 12 sts
Rounds 2–4: Knit.
Round 5: K2tog 6 times. 6 sts

Stuff stop lightly, break yarn, pull tail through remaining sts, knot, pull knot to inside of wheel. Press into shape.

Assemby

Sew buttons onto tongue, lining up with buttonholes (see figure 2).

Cut felt pieces using template. Sew black circle to yellow circle using thread, then attach to center of each wheel (see figure 3).

Sew wheels to bottom of skates (see figure 4). Sew toe stops to front ends of skates.

3

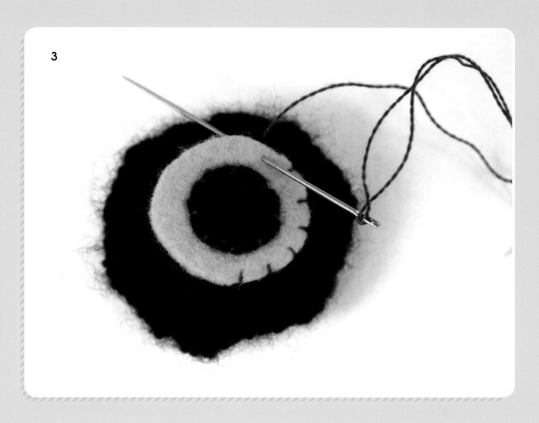

4

Yellow Wheel part (4)

Black Wheel part (4)

Baby Elf Shoes

I'm not sure why so many magical creatures wear shoes with curling toes, but they sure are cute. These tiny elf shoes aren't exactly magical, but it is magical how quickly you can knit them. The toes curl using a series of short row shaping, and the curling also allows the slippers to grow for a little longer with your baby. As for the pom poms, well how can you not love making pom poms?

Materials

- 1 skein Cascade 220 sport in 8903 lime green
- Small length of contrasting color yarn for pom pom
- US size 4 (3.5 mm) double pointed needles
- US size 6 (4.0 mm) double pointed needles (for cast on only)
- Stitch marker
- Yarn needle

Finished length:
0-3 mths – 3½ in.
6 mths – 4 in.
12 mths – 4½ in.

Gauge:
24 sts and 30 rows over
4in. in stockinette st

Glossary of abbreviations

CO – cast on
k – knit
k2tog – decrease by knitting
  two together
kfb – increase by knitting into front
  and back of stitch
p – purl
p2tog – decrease by purling
  two together
pm – place marker
st[s] – stitch[es]

Using US size 6 (4.0 mm) double pointed needles, CO30 [30, 32] sts Switch to US size 4 (3.5 mm) double pointed needles, place marker, join to knit in the round.
Round 1: (K1, p1) to end.
Repeat round 1 until cuff measures ¾ [3/4, 1] in.

Begin heel

Knit across 15 [15, 16] sts.
Leave remaining sts on one double pointed needle.
Turn and purl across 15 [15, 16] sts.
Next row: Slip 1 st purlwise, knit to end.
Next row: Slip 1 st purlwise, purl to end.
Repeat last 2 rows 3 [4, 5] more times (see figure 1).

Turn heel

Knit across 9 [9, 10] sts, ssk, k1, turn.
Slip 1 purlwise, p4 [5, 6], p2tog, p1, turn.
Slip 1 purlwise, knit to 1 st before gap, ssk, k1, turn.
Slip 1 purlwise, purl to 1 st before gap,

p2tog, p1, turn.
Knit to last 2 sts, ssk, turn.
Purl to last 2 sts, p2tog.

Connect to begin instep

With 1 double pointed needle, knit across heel sts, pick up and knit 7 [8, 9] sts along selvedge edge.
Using a second needle, knit across held sts on other needle.
Use a third needle to pick up and knit 7 [8, 9] sts from other selvedge edge. Pm, connect to knit in the round (see figure 2). 38 [40, 44] sts

Begin instep

Round 1: K14 [15, 17], k2tog, pm, k15 [15, 16], pm, ssk, k5 [6, 7].
Round 2: Knit.
Continue decreasing 1 st before each marker every other round until 30 [30, 32] sts remain.
Knit until sock measures 2 [2¼, 2½] in. from base of heel.
Next round: Ssk, k5 [5, 6], k2tog, k6)

twice. 26 [26, 28] sts
Knit 1 [2, 3] rounds even.
Next round: Ssk, k3 [3, 4], k2tog, k6)
twice. 22 [22, 24] sts
Knit 1 [2, 3] rounds even.

Turn toe

K5 [5, 6], ssk, k1, turn.
Slip 1 purlwise, p6 [6, 7], p2tog, p1, turn.
Slip 1 purlwise, knit to 1 st before gap, ssk, k1, turn.
Slip 1 purlwise, purl to 1 st before the gap, p2tog, p1, turn.
Repeat last 2 rounds until 16 [16, 18] sts remain.
Knit 2 [3, 4] rounds even.
Next round: K5 [5, 6], ssk, k1, turn.
Slip 1 purlwise, p6 [6, 7], p2tog, p1, turn.
Slip 1 purlwise, knit to 1 st before gap, ssk, k1, turn.
Slip 1 purlwise, purl to 1 st before the gap, p2tog, p1, turn, knit to marker.
12 [12, 14] sts
K3 [3, 4], ssk, k1, turn.
Slip 1 purlwise, p4 [4, 5], p2tog, p1, turn.

Slip 1 purlwise, knit to 1 st before gap, ssk, k1, turn.

Slip 1 purlwise, purl to 1 st before the gap, p2tog, p1, turn, knit to marker. 8 [8, 10] sts

K2tog 4 [4, 5] times. Break yarn, pull tail through remaining sts, weave tail into wrong side of sock. Block slippers.

Pom Pom

Follow instructions for making pom poms in the Hooter Hat pattern, but making this one 1 in. instead. Alternatively, you can easily buy pom poms and pom pom makers at any craft store. Sew pom pom to tip of slipper using matching yarn and yarn needle.

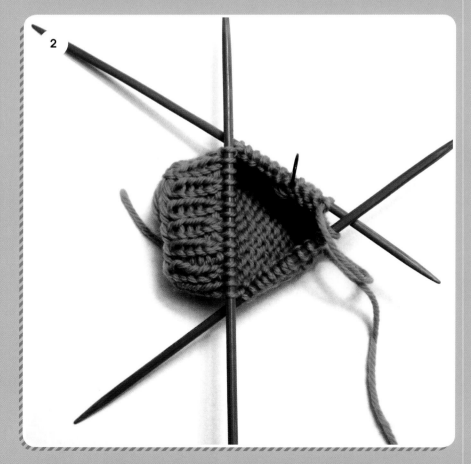

Raincloud Socks

Little kids love wearing rainboots, and why shouldn't they? They are easy to pull on, easy to clean with a hose, and perfect for jumping in streams and puddles. But I often find it difficult to find socks that are long enough to wear under the boots. So I thought, why not knit a pair? These socks are knit in the round with very soft Cherub DK. I used a duplicate stitch to create the graphic. Duplicate stitch is a wonderful tool for doing colorwork on things that are knit in the round. It's much simpler than fiddling with bobbins. It's also a great technique for adding color to a plain knitted object.

Materials

- 1 skein Cascade Cherub DK in 17 gray (MC)
- 1 skein Cascade Cherub DK in 28 blue (CC)
- 1 skein Cascade Cherub DK in 01 white
- US size 3 (3.25 mm) double pointed needles
- Stitch marker
- Yarn needle
- Sewing needle
- 4 small black buttons
- Dark gray embroidery floss

Finished foot circumference:
2-4 yrs – 5½ in.
4-8 yrs – 6½ in.
8 yrs/small adult – 7½ in.

Gauge:
24 sts and 30 rows over
4 in. in stockinette st

Glossary of abbreviations

CC – contrasting color
CO – cast on
k – knit
k2tog – decrease by knitting
    two together
MC – main color
p – purl
p2tog – decrease by purling
    two together
pm – place marker
sl – slip 1 stitch
ssk – decrease by slip one, slip one,
    knit slipped stitches together
st[s] – stitch[es]

Socks

Begin from top of calf:
Using MC, hold 2 double pointed needles together for a loose edge, and CO32 [40, 44] sts, pm, join to knit in the round.
Round 1: (K1, p1) to end.
Complete round 1, 4 [5, 6] more times.
Next round: Knit.
Knit even for 2 in.
Return to knitting k1, p1 ribbing. Work until sock measures 7 [8½, 10] in. from cast on edge.

Heel

Knit across 8 [10, 11] sts, turn and purl across 16 [20, 22] sts, leaving st marker in place.
Place remaining sts on 1 needle. Switch to CC. Begin knitting flat.

Row 1: (Sl 1 purlwise, k1). Repeat to end.
Row 2: Sl 1 purlwise, purl to end.
Repeat rows 1 and 2 until you have 16 [20, 22] heel rows.

Turn heel

Row 1: Knit across 10 [12, 13], ssk, k1, turn.
Row 2: Sl 1 purlwise, p5, p2tog, p1, turn.
Row 3: Sl 1 purlwise, knit to 1 st before gap, ssk, k1, turn.
Row 4: Sl 1 purlwise, purl to 1 st before gap, p2tog, p1, turn.
Repeat rows 3 and 4 until all heel sts have been worked and you have 10 [12, 14] sts remaining, ending in p2tog if necessary.

Heel gusset

Switch to MC.
With one needle, knit across all heel sts, pick up and knit 8 [10, 11] sts from edge of heel flap. With second needle, knit sts set aside on extra needle for instep, with 3rd needle, pick up and knit 8 [10, 11] sts from other edge of heel flap. Use the same needle to knit to marker (see figure 1).
42 [52, 58] sts
Round 1: Knit to last 3 sts on first needle, k2tog, k1, knit all sts from second needle, on the third needle, k1, ssk, knit to end.
40 [50, 56] sts
Round 2: Knit.
Repeat rounds 1 and 2 until you have 32 [40, 44] sts.
Knit even until the sock measure 4½ [5½, 6½] in. from back edge of heel, or 1 in. less than the desired length of foot.

Toe

Switch to CC.

Round 1: K5 [7, 8], k2tog, k2, ssk, k10 [14, 16], k2tog, k2, ssk, k5 [7, 8].
28 [36, 40] sts
Round 2: Knit.
Continue to decrease 4 sts every other round in this manner until you have 16 [20, 20] sts.
Decrease 4 sts on the next round.
12 [16, 16] sts
Use kitchener st to close up the toe hole (see figure 2). Weave in loose ends.

Duplicate stitch

Create cloud on socks using the chart as follows:

Fold sock in half, so that foot portion is flat. Complete the chart on the outside, being sure to do the left side on one sock, and the right side on the other.
Find the middle row. Count down 17 sts from the top, the count 5 sts to the right. This is the starting point for the chart, beginning with the bottom right edge of the white cloud.
Cut a 2 in. length of white yarn. Using a yarn needle, insert into the bottom of the V of the starting st (see figure 3).
Insert the needle through the stitch above (see figure 4). Pull yarn through gently, and insert needle back into bottom of V (see figure 5). Bring needle up through the V of the adjacent stitch (see figure 6). Repeat these steps until chart is completed.
Sew buttons into place for eyes (see figure 7).
Use a thick length of gray thread and couching st to outline the cloud and create frown, using a single strand to secure it into place (see figure 8).

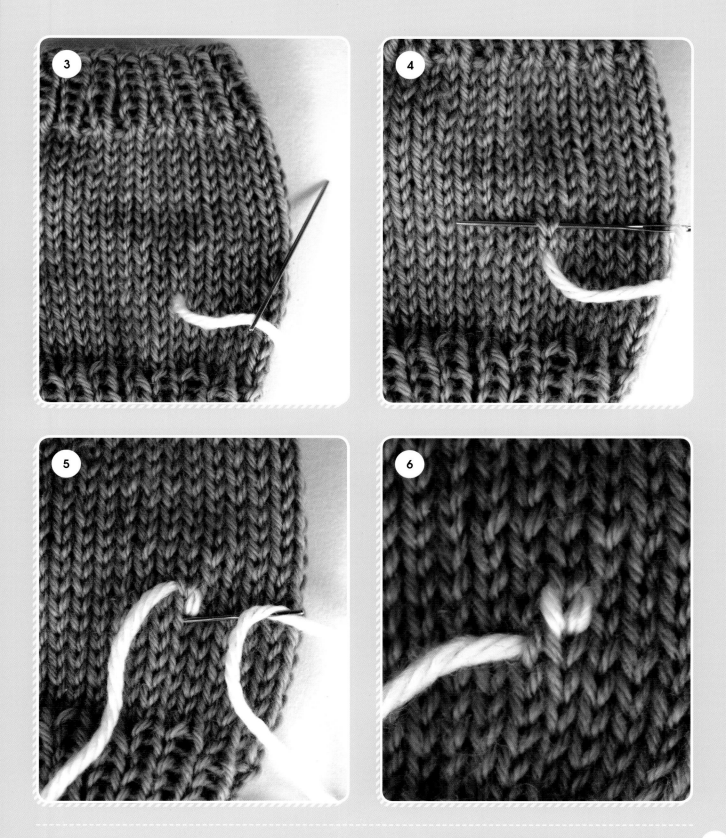

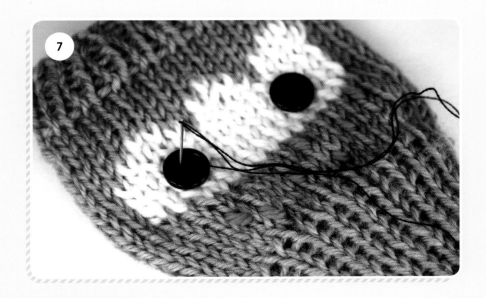

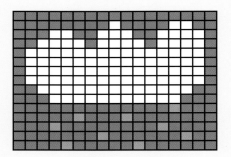

Knitting chart

Bug in a Rug Legwarmers

I suppose for most people, the idea of having your legs covered in bugs would be rather creepy. I'm not much of a fan of bugs in reality, quite the opposite in fact, but I do enjoy knitting them in colorful shades of wool. These legwarmers help make a bright and cozy transition from winter into spring. Perhaps it's still a little chilly to wear a skirt and bare your knees, but put on some legwarmers, and your skirt can be just a little bit shorter, or a lot shorter if that's your thing. The legwarmers are knit in the round, with stranded colorwork. They're a great project for using up remainders of various colors of yarn.

Materials

- 1 skein Cascade 220 in 8010 off white
- 1 skein Cascade 220 in 9430 dark green
- 1 skein Cascade 220 in 9468 blue
- 1 skein Cascade 220 in 9466 red
- 1 skein Cascade 220 in 8903 bright green
- 1 skein Cascade 220 in 9542 orange
- US size 7 (4.5 mm) 18 in. circular needle
- 1 set US size 7 (4.5 mm) double pointed needles
- 1 set US size 5 (3.75 mm) double pointed needles
- Stitch markers
- Yarn needle
- 4 red buttons: ½ in.

Finished size:
14½ in. long (can be adjusted)

Gauge:
22 sts and 26 rows over 4 in. in stockinette st

Glossary of abbreviations

CO – cast on
dbl yo – double yarn over
k – knit
k2tog – decrease by knitting two together
kfb – increase by knitting into front and back of stitch
p – purl
pm – place marker
st[s] – stitch[es]

Legwarmers

Begin at bottom edge (make 2).
Note: When knitting second legwarmer, create buttonholes on the opposite edge.
Using US size 7 (4.5 mm) circular needle and off white, CO58.
Row 1: (K1, p1) to end.
Row 2: (P1, k1) twice, (k1, p1) to last 4 sts, (p1, k1) twice.
Row 3: K2tog, dbl yo, k2tog, (k1, p1) to end.
Row 4: (P1, k1) twice, pm, knit to last 4 sts, pm, (p1, k1) twice.
Row 5: (K1, p1) twice, begin chart 1 with a purl row, repeating 5 times between markers, (k1, p1) twice.
Continue knitting chart with seed stitch border on sides until chart is complete. Make one additional buttonhole on the 9th row.
Next row: (P1, k1) twice, knit to next marker. Connect edges as follows:
Place each of the first 4 sts and the last 4 sts on two US size 7 (4.5 mm) double pointed needles. Overlap so that the buttonholes are on top. Knit the first st from the top needle together with the first st from the second needle. Repeat with the remaining 6 sts (see figure 1). Remove first marker. Knit to second marker, dividing sts on double pointed needles as you go. This marker now marks the beginning of the round (see figure 2). 54 sts
Knit 2 rounds.

Begin knitting chart 2, repeating 6 times each round.
Knit 1 round.
Next round: (Kfb, k8) 6 times. 60 sts
Knit 1 round.

Begin chart 3, repeating 5 times each round.
Knit 1 round.
Next round: (Kfb, k9) 6 times. 66 sts
Knit 1 round.

Begin chart 4, repeating 6 times
each round.
Knit 1 round.
Next round: (K2tog, k64). 65 sts
Knit 1 round.

Begin chart 5, repeating 5 times
each round.
Knit 1 round.
Switch to US size 5 (3.75 mm) double
pointed needles.
Next round: (K1, p1) to last stitch, k1.
Repeat last round 3 more times, or until
desired length. Bind off loosely in pattern.
Weave in loose ends. Block well.
Sew buttons, lining up with buttonholes
(see figure 3).

3

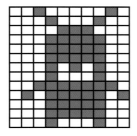

Knitting chart 1

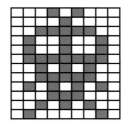

Knitting chart 2

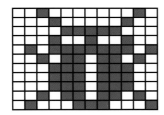

Knitting chart 3

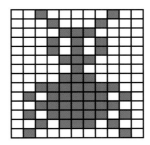

Knitting chart 4

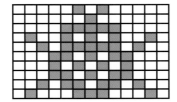

Knitting chart 5

Bigfoot Slippers

I really love being barefoot. Unfortunately, it's too cold three-quarters of the year here to enjoy feeling the grass between your toes. This is what inspired me to knit the Bigfoot Slippers. I thought it would be funny to have bedroom slippers that look like feet. Then I realized it would be even funnier to have slippers that look like gigantic feet. They're also quite funny for dancing, in a slightly dangerous sort of way.

Materials

- 2 skeins Cascade 220 in 8021 beige
- 1 set US size 6 (4.0 mm) double pointed needles
- 1 US size 6 (4.0 mm) circular needle, 16in. (optional)
- Stitch markers
- Yarn needle
- Embroidery needle
- Toy stuffing
- 2in. thick foam pad (any chair pad from craft store will do)
- 1 yard polar fleece fabric in white for lining (or color of choice)
- 1 piece of off white felt
- Off white thread
- Fabric marker

Finished size:
15 in. long

Gauge:
18 sts and 24 rows over
4in. in stockinette st

Glossary of abbreviations

BO – bind off
CO – cast on
k – knit
k2tog – decrease by knitting two together
kfb – increase by knitting into front and back of stitch
p – purl
p2tog – decrease by purling two together
pm – place marker
ssk – decrease by slip one, slip one, knit slipped stitches together
st[s] – stitch[es]

Note: *For children and a smaller size, use Cascade 220 sport weight and US size 5 (3.75 mm) needles. For large men's feet, use Cascade 220 Chunky and US size 9 (5.5 mm) needles.

Right foot

Using double pointed needles, *CO6, pm, join to knit in the round.
Round 1: Kfb 6 times. 12 sts
Round 2 and all even rounds through round 18: Knit.
Round 3: (Kfb, k1) 6 times. 18 sts
Round 5: (Kfb, k2) 6 times. 24 sts
Round 7: (Kfb, k3) 6 times. 30 sts
Round 9: (Kfb, k2, kfb twice, k9, kfb) twice. 38 sts
Round 11: (Kfb, k4, kfb twice, k11, kfb) twice. 46 sts
Round 13: (Kfb, k6, kfb twice, k13, kfb) twice. 54 sts
Round 15: (Kfb, k8, kfb twice, k15, kfb) twice. 62 sts

Round 17: (K12, kfb, k17, kfb) twice. 66 sts
Begin dividing sts for foot hole. Be sure to keep stitch marker in place for later:
Row 19: K19, BO7, k59 (you will pass marker), turn (see figure 1). 59 sts
Row 20: P2tog, p55, p2tog. 57 sts
Row 21: K2tog, k3, kfb, k12, kfb, k19, kfb, k12, kfb, k3, ssk. 59 sts
Row 22: Purl.
Row 23: K2tog, k47, ssk. 57 sts
Row 24–30: Complete in stockinette st.
Row 31: Kfb, k47, kfb. 59 sts
Row 32: Purl.*
Row 33: Kfb, k3, ssk, k12, k2tog, k38, kfb.
Row 34: Purl.
Complete the last two rounds twice more.

Next row: K59, CO5. Rejoin to knit in the round. Knit to marker. 64 sts
Round 40: K30, ssk, k12, k2tog, k18. 62 sts
Rounds 41–45: Knit.
Round 46: (K12, kfb, k17, kfb) twice. 66 sts
Rounds 47–48: Knit.
Round 49: (K12, kfb, k19, kfb) twice. 70 sts
Rounds 50–51: Knit.
Round 52: (K12, kfb, k21, kfb) twice. 74 sts
Rounds 53–54: Knit.
Round 55: (K12, kfb, k23, kfb) twice. 78 sts
Rounds 56–57: Knit.

Round 58: (K12, kfb, k25, kfb) twice. 82 sts
Rounds 59–60: Knit.
Round 61: K40, kfb, k12, kfb, k28. 84 sts
Round 62: K41, kfb, k12, kfb, k29. 86 sts
Round 63: K42, kfb, k12, kfb, k30. 88 sts
Round 64: K43, kfb, k12, kfb, k31. 90 sts
Round 65: K44, kfb, k12, kfb, k32. 92 sts
Rounds 66–79: Knit.
Round 80: K2tog, k54, ssk, k34. 90 sts
Round 81: K2tog, k52, ssk, k34. 88 sts
Round 82: K2tog, k50, ssk, k34. 86 sts
Round 83: K2tog, k48, ssk, k34. 84 sts
Round 84: K2tog, k6, k2tog, k30, ssk, k6, ssk, k2tog, k30, ssk. 78 sts
Round 85: (K2tog, k3, ssk, k2tog, k28, ssk) twice. 70 sts
Leave yarn attached. Place all sts on a piece of contrasting scrap yarn.

Begin dividing for toes
Little toe
Starting where the yarn connects, pick up and knit 5 sts on the first needle for the outside of toe, pick up and knit the next 5 sts on second needle for front of toe, using a third needle CO5, with fourth needle pick up and knit 5 sts from the back for the bottom of the toe. Place marker, join to knit in the round (see figure 2). 20 sts
Rounds 1–4: Knit.
Round 5: K5, kfb, k3, kfb, k5, kfb, k3, kfb. 24 sts
Rounds 6–9: Knit.
Round 10: (K2tog, k2) 6 times. 18 sts
Round 11: Knit.
Round 12: (K2tog, k1) 6 times. 12 sts
Round 13: K2tog 6 times. 6 sts
Break yarn, pull tail through remaining sts, knot, pull to inside of toe.

Fourth toe
Beginning at back outside of little toe, pick up and knit 5 sts along the base, using second needle pick up and knit 5 sts from front of foot, with third needle, CO5 sts, with fourth needle, pick up and knit next 5 sts on bottom of foot. Place marker, join to knit in the round (see figure 3). 20 sts
Rounds 1–6: Knit.
Round 7: K5, kfb, k3, kfb, k5, kfb, k3, kfb. 24 sts
Rounds 8–11: Knit.
Round 12: (K2tog, k2) 6 times. 18 sts
Round 13: Knit.
Round 14: (K2tog, k1) 6 times. 12 sts
Round 15: K2tog 6 times. 6 sts
Break yarn, pull tail through remaining sts, knot, pull to inside of toe.

Third toe
Beginning at back outside of little toe, pick up and knit 5 sts along the base, using second needle pick up and knit 6 sts from front of foot, with third needle, CO5 sts, with fourth needle, pick up and knit next 6 sts on bottom of foot. Place marker, join to knit in the round. 22 sts
Rounds 1–8: Knit.
Round 9: K5, kfb, k4, kfb, k5, kfb, k4, kfb. 26 sts
Rounds 10–13: Knit.
Round 14: K5, k2tog, k4, k2tog, k13. 24 sts

1

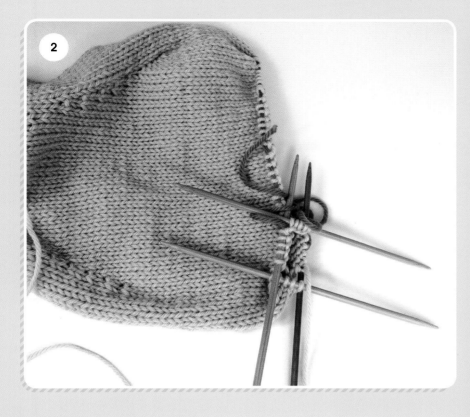

Round 15: (K2tog, k2) 6 times. 18 sts
Round 16: Knit.
Round 17: (K2tog, k1) 6 times. 12 sts
Round 18: K2tog 6 times. 6 sts
Break yarn, pull tail through remaining sts, knot, pull to inside of toe.

Second toe
Beginning at back outside of little toe, pick up and knit 5 sts along the base, using second needle pick up and knit 6 sts from front of foot, with third needle, CO5 sts, with fourth needle, pick up and knit next 6 sts on bottom of foot. Place marker, join to knit in the round. 22 sts
Rounds 1–9: Knit.
Round 10: (K5, kfb, k4, kfb) twice. 26 sts
Round 11: (K5, k fb, k6, k fb) twice. 30 sts
Rounds 12–15: Knit.
Round 16: (K2tog, k3) 6 times. 24 sts
Round 17: Knit.
Round 18: (K2tog, k2) 6 times. 18 sts
Round 19: Knit.
Round 20: (K2tog, k1) 6 times. 12 sts
Round 21: K2tog 6 times. 6 sts
Break yarn, pull tail through remaining sts, knot, pull to inside of toe.

Big toe
Beginning at back outside of little toe, pick up and knit 5 sts along the base, using second needle pick up and knit 8 sts from front of foot, with third needle, pick up and knit 5 sts from outside edge of foot, with fourth needle, pick up and knit remaining 8 sts on bottom of foot. Place marker, join to knit in the round. 26 sts
Rounds 1–2: Knit.
Round 3: Kfb, k4, kfb, k6, kfb, k4, kfb twice, k6, kfb. 32 sts
Round 4: Knit.
Round 5: Kfb, k5, kfb, k8, kfb, k5, kfb twice, k8, k fb. 38 sts
Rounds 6–11: Knit.
Round 12: K26, k2tog, k8, k2tog. 36 sts
Round 13: Knit.
Round 14: (K2tog, k4) 6 times. 30 sts
Round 15: Knit.
Round 16: (K2tog, k3) 6 times. 24 sts
Round 17: Knit.

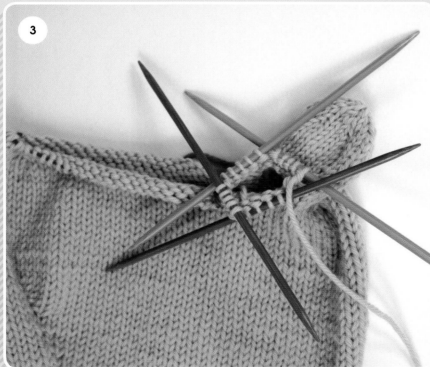

Round 18: (K2tog, k2) 6 times. 18 sts
Round 19: Knit.
Round 20: (K2tog, k1) 6 times. 12 sts
Round 21: K2tog 6 times. 6 sts
Break yarn, pull tail through remaining sts, knot, pull to inside of toe.

Left foot
Complete as for right foot from * to *.
Row 33: Kfb, k38, ssk, k10, k2tog, k3, kfb.
Row 34: Purl.
Complete the last two rounds twice more.
Next row: K59, CO5. Rejoin to knit in the round. Knit to marker. 64 sts
Round 40: K12, k2tog, k48, ssk. 62 sts
Rounds 41–45: Knit.
Round 46: (K12, kfb, k17, kfb) twice. 66 sts
Rounds 47–48: Knit.
Round 49: (K12, kfb, k19, kfb) twice. 70 sts
Rounds 50–51: Knit.
Round 52: (K12, kfb, k21, kfb) twice. 74 sts
Rounds 53–54: Knit.
Round 55: (K12, kfb, k23, kfb) twice. 78 sts
Rounds 56–57: Knit.
Round 58: (K12, kfb, k25, kfb) twice. 82 sts
Rounds 59–60: Knit.
Round 61: K12, kfb, k63, kfb. 84 sts
Round 62: K12, kfb, k65, kfb. 86 sts
Round 63: K12, kfb, k67, kfb. 88 sts
Round 64: K12, kfb, k69, kfb. 90 sts
Round 65: K12, kfb, k71, kfb. 92 sts
Rounds 66–79: Knit.
Round 80: K2tog, k54, ssk, k34. 90 sts
Round 81: K2tog, k52, ssk, k34. 88 sts
Round 82: K2tog, k50, ssk, k34. 86 sts
Round 83: K2tog, k48, ssk, k34. 84 sts
Round 84: K2tog, k6, k2tog, k30, ssk, k6, ssk, k2tog, k30, ssk. 78 sts
Round 85: (K2tog, k3, ssk, k2tog, k28, ssk) twice. 70 sts
Leave yarn attached. Place all sts on a piece of contrasting scrap yarn.

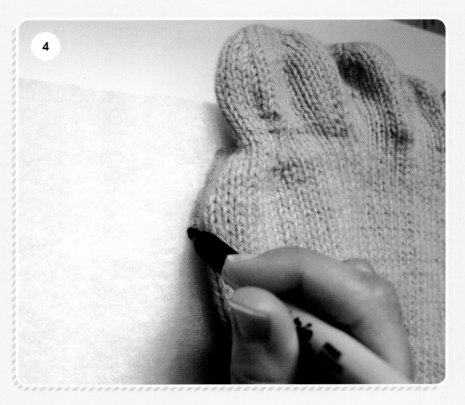

Begin dividing for toes

Big toe

Starting where the yarn connects, pick up and knit 5 sts on the first needle for the outside of toe, pick up and knit the next 8 sts on second needle for front of toe, using a third needle CO5, with fourth needle pick up and knit 8 sts from the back for the bottom of the toe. Place marker, join to knit in the round. 26 sts Complete same as for big toe on right foot.

Second toe

Beginning at back outside of first toe, pick up and knit 5 sts along the base, using second needle pick up and knit 6 sts from front of foot, with third needle, pick up and knit 5 sts from outside edge of foot, with fourth needle, pick up and knit next 6 sts on bottom of foot. Place marker, join to knit in the round. 22 sts Complete same as for second toe on right foot.

Third toe

Beginning at back outside of second toe, pick up and knit 5 sts along the base, using second needle pick up and knit 6 sts from front of foot, with third needle, pick up and knit 5 sts from outside edge of foot, with fourth needle, pick up and knit next 6 sts on bottom of foot. Place marker, join to knit in the round. 22 sts Complete same as for third toe on right foot.

Fourth toe

Beginning at back outside of third toe, pick up and knit 5 sts along the base, using second needle pick up and knit 5 sts from front of foot, with third needle, pick up and knit 5 sts from outside edge of foot, with fourth needle, pick up and knit next 5 sts on bottom of foot. Place marker, join to knit in the round. 20 sts Complete same as for fourth toe on right foot.

Little toe

Beginning at back outside of fourth toe, pick up and knit 5 sts along the base, using second needle pick up and knit 5 sts from front of foot, with third needle, pick up and knit 5 sts from outside edge of foot, with fourth needle, pick up and knit 5 remaining sts on scrap yarn. Place marker, join to knit in the round. 20 sts Complete same as for little toe on right foot.
Weave in all loose ends. Block feet.

Assemby

Lay one foot flat one top of the foam pad. Using a washable marker, begin at the base of the toes and trace around bottom edge, stopping at the base of the toes on the other side (see figure 4). Pick up foot. Use marker to connect edges of the tracing in a straight line (see figure 5). Use a sharp pair of scissors or an X-acto knife to cut out the foot, just inside the marker line (see figure 6). If the pad is thick, it may be helpful cut around the edge one layer at a time. The edges do not need to be neat as they will be hidden.

Trace the first foam foot onto another piece of foam, and cut out the second foot pad. Insert foam pads into knitted feet by rolling up and stuffing through the opening. Trim pads as needed to fit. Remove pads from knitted feet. Stuff toes firmly.

Lay foam feet on top of the fleece fabric. Use a fabric marker to trace and cut 4 pieces for slipper lining (see figure 7). Into each knitted foot, insert first a foam piece, and then 2 cut pieces of fleece. Smooth to even out. Use the marker to trace slipper opening onto the top piece of fleece (see figure 8).

Remove fleece from slippers. Cut out opening in the top layer of fleece from each slipper. Sew two layers together around outside perimeter, either by hand, or with a sewing machine (see figure 9). Slide fleece lining back into slipper, on top of foam layer. Smooth, matching opening in fleece to opening in knitted fabric. Sew around the perimeter of the slipper using thread (see figure 10), stopping halfway. Stuff foot lightly along the top to give it the desired shape (see figure 11).

Cut toenails from felt using templates. Sew onto tops of toes using thread (see figure 12).

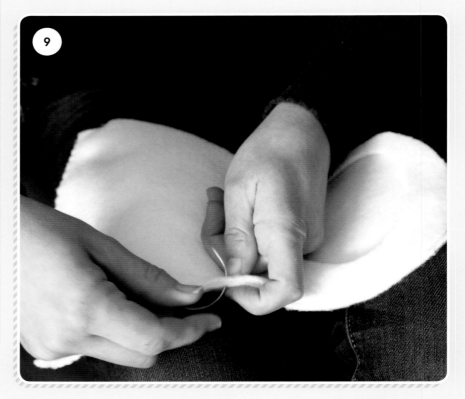

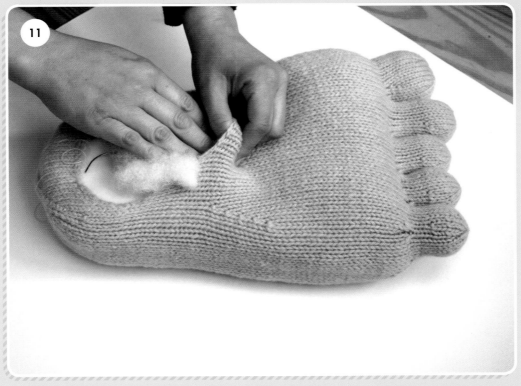

12

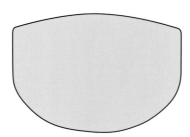

Big toenail (2)

Little toenail (8)

Difficulty Key and Acknowledgments

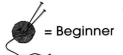 = Beginner    = Intermediate    = Seasoned

Cascade is a manufacturer and international distributor of fine yarns, their products are available worldwide. I thank them for supplying all the yarns used in this book.

In the late 1980s, Bob and Jean Dunbabin founded Cascade Yarns in Seattle, Washington with the goal to provide affordable, high-quality yarns. The search for a soft, long-stapled wool brought Bob Dunbabin to Peru, where he found plentiful, light-colored, high lofting wool from sheep (a hybrid of the native Corriedale and Merino) that were raised by Peruvian natives in the Sierra Mountains above 12,000 feet. Largely by word-of-mouth, Cascade 220 became renowned as the affordable high-quality knitting yarn with great yardage that is available in more than 350 Solids, Heathers, Quatros, Tweeds, and Hand Paints.

Model List:

Accordion Handwarmer- Chloe Paddison, *Baby Bird Dress-* Grace Scantlin, *Badger Scarf-* David Brewer, *Barnyard Buddies-* Giorgie Martinez, *Bigfoot Slippers-* Gregory Beddingfield, *Bluetooth Hat-* Beckett Summerville, *Bug in a Rug Legwarmers-* Katie Boyette, *Cyclops Friends Mittens-* Sophia Park, *Feed Me! Bib-* Grace Scantlin, *Grump Sweater-* Simon Westbrook, *Hooter Hat-* Katie Boyette, *Lobster Claw Mittens-* Beckett Summerville, *Mr. Micro Charm-* Chloe Paddison, *Ninja Mitts-* Katie Boyette, *Raincloud Socks-* Sophia Park, *Robot Love Scarf-* Drew Boyette, *Save the Yeti Scarf-* Chloe Paddison, *Shark Bait Sweater-* Sylvie Kaminsky

Also available from Katie Boyette

Knits on the following pages in *Wearable KnitWits* can be found in Katie's first book *KnitWit:*
Pg 66 Otto
Pg 79 Jacques Crusteau
Pg 87 Ninja
Pg 127 Mr. Abominable

Knits on the following pages in *Wearable KnitWits* can be found in Katie's second book *More KnitWits:*
Pg 43 Rutentuten
Pg 47 Clink
Pg 71 Joe and Cornelius
Pg 93 Babushka
Pg 105 Pickle
Pg 116 Matilda

KnitWit
ISBN: 978-1-4162-0608-8

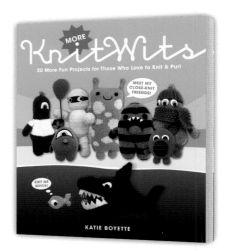

More KnitWits
ISBN 978-1-4162-0644-6